Beyond the 401(k)

*Helping Employees
Achieve Total
Financial Security*

INVESTORS
PRESS

Published in the United States by Investors Press, Inc.

Library of Congress Cataloging-in-Publication Data

Investors Press, Inc.

Beyond the 401(k)
Helping Employees Achieve Total Financial Security

ISBN 1-885123-12-4

I. Beyond the 401(k)
Helping Employees Achieve Total Financial Security

Printed in the United States
10 9 8 7 6 5 4 3 2 1

Jacket illustration by Michael Gibbs
Book and jacket design by Silver Communications Inc., New York

ACKNOWLEDGEMENT

Investors Press is pleased to present **Beyond the 401(k):** *Helping Employees Achieve Total Financial Security.*

Each book in our ongoing Investment Management Series examines important issues of compelling concern to pension and investment officers, trustees, benefits administrators, pension consultants and money managers. Written by distinguished plan sponsors, each case study reflects their individual experience, independent opinions and informed insights.

Published by Investors Press, this unique educational series is made possible by the support and participation of a select group of leading firms to whom appreciation goes from everyone who values the importance of education and the candid exchange of information. Because of their commitment, these books are valuable tools that encourage industry-wide dialogue, discussion and deeper understanding.

INVESTORS
PRESS

Beyond the 401(k)

Helping Employees Achieve Total Financial Security

Underwritten by

ALLMERICA FINANCIAL INSTITUTIONAL SERVICES

AMERICAN CENTURY$_{\text{SM}}$ INVESTMENTS

AMERICAN EXPRESS FINANCIAL ADVISORS INC.

FOUNDERS ASSET MANAGEMENT, INC.

JOHN HANCOCK FUNDS

KEYCORP

MERRILL LYNCH & CO.

METLIFE

ROGERS, CASEY & ASSOCIATES, INC.

SCUDDER INVESTOR SERVICES, INC.

TABLE OF CONTENTS

Not long ago, Patricia Haverland, pension and investment director of The Black & Decker Corp., surveyed the company's 19,000 employees about their 401(k) plan. "How many funds would you prefer?" she asked. "How important is it to be able to find your investments listed in the newspapers? If you don't participate in the plan, why not?"

She read their responses with great interest. "It was in the additional comments and questions section that the real surprise came," she says. "It became clear to me that many of our employees don't understand what a savings plan is, let alone a stock or a bond." Now Haverland and her colleagues are developing a more comprehensive program to teach employees the basics.

What would you do in Haverland's position? It's not a casual question. In fact, chances are that if you were to do a little digging, you'd find similar results among your own employees. Consider a 1995 study of 803 401(k) participants by the John Hancock Mutual Life Insurance Co. in Boston. Thirty-five percent of respondents thought it is impossible to lose money in a bond fund; 56% felt that money market funds will outperform stable value funds over a 10-year period; and 87% were unaware that money market funds are backed by short-term securities. John Hancock's survey revealed much the same reality Haverland discovered: employees sorely lack much of the most basic investment and financial planning knowledge they need to become successful investors and savers.

It is this knowledge gap that drives today's heated debate within the pensions community on two controversial issues: who is responsible for employee financial education and to what extent? Indeed, if the 401(k) is just one piece of the financial puzzle, should employers help their employees understand the bigger picture? Have companies, in fact, left out the crucial first step in their financial education efforts? Without basic, general financial education, will employees be able to take full advantage of their 401(k) plans—and is providing that education the company's responsibility?

"Hello, Mary Smith in Department 25? My records tell me that you have maxed out on your VISA, MasterCard and American Express—and last month you went out to dinner fourteen times!"

The Arguments Against

A significant number of plan sponsors are unwilling to expand the educational role they have traditionally played. They are comfortable providing nuts-and-bolts information about their plan: what the options are and how employees can benefit from investing in a tax-deferred savings vehicle. Most of these "traditionalists" simply don't think it's appropriate to take on the bigger task of total financial education and question whether it is, in fact, necessary.

The MidAmerican Energy Company in Des Moines, Iowa, for example, whose plan has assets of $200 million, addresses financial and investment basics in its 401(k) enrollment packages. Thomas Foster, finance and investment administrator, explains that although one of his company's major objectives is to encourage employees to diversify their investments and avoid market timing, "We've made the assumption that employees have a general understanding of how to manage their finances and we don't need to micromanage their household budget." Despite Foster's intuition that the majority of employees do not fully understand the concept of diversification and are more risk-averse than they need to be, he maintains that they are making decisions according to their individual risk profiles.

Many other plan sponsors agree with Foster and question where they should draw the line. How does a company decide exactly how far its responsibility to educate goes? Does it extend to getting a mortgage? Buying a car? One plan sponsor at a multinational company with over 30,000 employees and both a defined benefit and defined contribution plan puts it this way: "We can't fix everything. Are we responsible for teaching employees about life insurance, too? Most people don't have a clue about that and are underinsured. You can educate and educate, but it's still up to the employees to take action."

For businesses with considerable turnover or employees working in disparate locations, it often comes down to a matter of logistics. Spartanburg, South Carolina-based Flagstar Corp., operator of six restaurant chains including Denny's, has 10,000 participants in its two 401(k) plans, with combined assets of $163.5 million. Its locations are spread out over 42 states and many have only ten eligible employees. For that reason, says Lee Holliday, director of retirement and savings, holding in-depth educational meetings is next to impossible. He has hired an outside company to develop a booklet and a video about the plan, which recently expanded the number of its investment options to eight. But he probably won't do much more than that.

THE OTHER SIDE

Notwithstanding the resistance of the traditionalists, more and more plan sponsors are beginning to accept the idea that their responsibility to employees includes offering broader financial educational programs. Moreover, they see that responsibility in several different ways:

> **Legal and fiduciary:** Under ERISA, employers must provide employees with enough information to make informed decisions about their 401(k), but they cannot give investment advice. In a 1996 Interpretive Bulletin, the Department of Labor issued new rules that qualify how companies can educate employees about their 401(k) investments without exposing themselves to fiduciary liability as an investment advisor.

The new rules stipulate that employers can provide information about the plan, such as benefits of participation and historical performance, general financial information about investment concepts like risk and return and diversification, and asset allocation models. The new rules help, but not enough. In fact, many plan sponsors are still concerned that they could be sued for giving inadequate information. They continue to ask themselves "Can employees come back years later to blame the company if, for example, their 401(k) investment choices failed to provide the kind of retirement income they expected?"

For a growing number of plan sponsors, the answer is to develop more in-depth educational programs. "Our attorneys advised that we have more to worry about if we don't give enough education than if we give too much," says Paul Avalone, senior director of human resources at Hyperion Software, a Stamford, Connecticut company whose 401(k) plan has $20 million in assets. By teaching employees the fundamentals they need to know about finance, Hyperion hopes to protect itself from future liability and provide the kind of education that fulfills its fiduciary responsibilities to its employees.

> **Corporate:** To many plan sponsors, more education just makes good business sense. For starters, it can provide a unique competitive advantage by helping companies attract top-notch employees, particularly in high-tech companies who need sophisticated, well-educated people. "We are in an extremely competitive market and our company is growing very fast," says Avalone. "If you want to be a cutting-edge employer you have to provide cutting-edge benefits." Sally Brewster, benefits manager for Apple Computer in Cupertino, California agrees. "Offering a broader range of educational programs reinforces the perception of us as a leading-edge

company. It makes us an employer of choice."

Expanded financial education can also affect the bottom line. Why? Employees burdened by financial worries—credit card debt, confusion about how to pay for their children's' college education or a new car or house—are likely to be less productive than those who have personal money management issues under control.

According to financial psychology expert Kathleen Gurney, Ph.D., the shift in the U.S. business environment from corporate paternalism to individual employee responsibility for lifelong financial planning has heightened anxiety in workers, producing greater stress and a sense of lost control because of increased job and retirement insecurity. Such insecurity can interfere with their ability to concentrate and the degree of responsibility they assume for their work. In extreme cases, some workers may become severely depressed or incapacitated if they don't see the possibility of solving their financial problems. Gurney emphasizes the positive power of expanded education as a way to help workers regain a sense of self-determination—their ability to feel in control of their financial destiny.

➤ **Moral:** For some plan sponsors the fact that employees aren't equipped to deal with financial matters or able to understand how to get the biggest benefit from their 401(k) means one thing: they have a moral responsibility to do more to help. That's particularly true in companies where the defined contribution plan is the only game in town.

Consider Apple Computer. Its 401(k), with $360 million in assets, is the sole retirement vehicle offered to employees. Brewster is adamant when she says, "It's not fair to hand people the responsibility for saving without giving them the tools they need to make the right choices. It's like giving the right to vote without providing enough information about the issues, then chastising people for not casting a ballot."

An informal survey of more than 100 Investors Press plan sponsor readers across the country shows that a majority agrees with Brewster. Sixty-six percent of the respondents think employers have a responsibility to educate employees beyond the 401(k) to ensure their total financial security. Forty-four percent offer retirement planning, 10% educate employees about basic money management and 17% offer employees financial planning. Thirty-three percent offer employees all of those things. Of those companies offering expanded financial educational programs, more than half (65%) offer them to all employees, not just 401(k) participants. In addition, 63% of respondents open their programs to spouses.

DIFFERENT STROKES

There's no one-size-fits-all solution when it comes to offering broader financial education. Thanks to everything from employee age to staff size and management philosophy, what's appropriate for one business may not be right for another—and companies are at very different stages in their planning efforts.

Some companies still want to focus their education on issues related to retirement planning but mix in a heavy dose of basic investment information. Ron Samuels, employee benefits specialist for the Nashville, Tennessee-based Baptist Sunday School Board, oversees a 401(k), a 403(b) and a defined benefits plan. He is currently mulling over what such a program would look like at his organization and considering one-hour seminars during brown bag lunches that would begin by convincing employees of the need to save for retirement and finish by explaining the core principles of investing required to save wisely.

At Acme Metals in Riverdale, Illinois, benefits and compensation manager Scott Brown has several reasons to emphasize retirement planning in educational programs. The company's retirement savings plans are complicated and many employees need a helping hand to understand how they work. The company contributes 7.5% of pay for each employee who participates in its 401(k), whether or not the participant contributes, and allows a maximum contribution of 10% of pay. Acme also has an ESOP, into which the company contributes 3% of pay. Since the average age of Acme employees is 46, and most tend to invest heavily in conservative money market funds, Brown sees a special responsibility to educate them before it's too late.

The company recently changed its recordkeeper and trustee and increased the number of investment options to seven from four, including four equity funds. Brown decided that was the time to provide more education. The new trustee ran a 75-minute class during work hours, covering such topics as how stocks perform over time, how bonds work and how to understand the concepts of risk vs. reward. Response was good: 85% of employees attended. He hopes to follow-up with another round of meetings next year.

Other companies are starting, or at least thinking about starting, a more comprehensive curriculum. At Apple Computer, Brewster is in the early stages of putting together her own program. She wants to expand the company's 401(k) information meetings so it has something for everyone. With that goal in mind, she plans to offer a range of seminars conducted by third-party experts covering subjects like tax planning and budgeting, all the way up to how to develop a soup-to-nuts financial plan. Apple will supplement those classes by expanding the company's Intranet network, over which employees can access a wide range of financial information from a variety of mutual fund companies and brokerage houses.

Montell USA in Wilmington, Delaware, is going full speed ahead with its program. In September 1995, Anne St. Clair, manager of benefit trust, launched a one-hour, monthly lunch-time seminar that ran for nine months. She calls the program "Financial Planning 101". One meeting covered fixed-income instruments, another how to save for college, a third mutual funds. Only one class focused on the 401(k) plan.

After the classes were over, a few things happened. First, employees responded with great enthusiasm. Especially important to St. Clair was not just the fact that people were happy with the sessions, but that it was clear they wanted more. "People wanted us to bring them to the next level," she says. Second, the company revamped its plan, adding three more investment options to the four it had offered. St. Clair decided to expand the classes. In October 1996, she initiated an eight-month program to provide a more detailed look at the plan's investment choices that included more advanced financial material. Each investment option was the topic of its own class. In early 1997, chief economists from two banks presented current analyses of the economy. Subsequent seminars focused on sophisticated topics, including investing in international stocks.

As can be expected with any experiment, these forays into educational expansion aren't always successful. When Dayton Hudson ran a two-hour evening program on basic issues like budgeting, financing a car and basic retirement planning, employee attendance and response were lukewarm. Despite the fact that Dayton Hudson promoted the program, employees seemed uninterested in classes and were not willing to attend them in the evening. For the moment, the company doesn't have plans to try other classes. "They don't seem to be the answer here," notes benefit accounting analyst Carol Wooten. She and her colleagues are figuring out what their next step should be.

NITTY GRITTY ISSUES

As Wooten's experience shows, there's no clear road map to follow when planning a broader financial education program. You can expect to face many complicated issues, including:

1. Footing the Bill

The best program in the world won't get off the drawing board unless there's money to pay for it. But most companies have limited resources for special classes or seminars, especially in these cost-conscious times. "I think we have a responsibility to do whatever we can to educate our participants, but it has to be within our resources," says Wooten.

Financial resources aren't the only problem. Many benefits departments lack the staff to get the ball rolling. "Right now we're working on so many things—merging our recordkeeping for both our 401(k) and defined benefits plan and changing trustees—we don't have the ability to do more," notes Wooten. The Baptist Sunday School Board is another case in point. With a benefits team of only two full-time and one part-time staff members overseeing medical, life insurance and retirement benefits for 1,725 employees and 1,200 retirees, it is understandable that no one has had the time to develop additional educational programs.

What can companies do? A cost-effective and trouble-free solution is to use outside vendors, like brokerage firms, to conduct classes for free. Many of the plan sponsors who responded to the informal Investors Press survey agree. Forty-five percent use third-party specialists for all their financial education, including 401(k) education; 40% use their 401(k) service provider and 26% use in-house counselors.

The trouble is, you can expect plenty of strings to be attached. "Brokerage houses will fall all over themselves to do it for no charge, but there's a conflict of interest," says Avalone of Hyperion Software. "They'll use the opportunity to sell their own products." Plus, you'll still have to devote considerable resources to shopping for the best vendor, advertising the program and supervising it.

Still, you can minimize some of those problems by carefully discussing beforehand exactly what the vendor expects to get out of the program and insisting on a soft-sell-only approach. At Montell, St. Clair arranged for classes to be taught for free by the plan's investment managers, as well as by financial planners. "When we introduced the instructors, we told employees they could take advantage of a complimentary consultation," she says. "Not everyone did, but I think those who followed through were pleased with the service."

Another option is to hire an outside vendor who doesn't sell anything. In that case, however, you'll have to pay. To lessen your costs, you can charge employees for all or part of the program, or for the cost of materials. There's an added benefit to that approach, according to Karen Stecher, benefits manager for Blue-Cross Blue-Shield. "It shows that employees are interested enough to contribute something of their own into their education," she says.

Interestingly, 54% of the respondents to the Investors Press survey say their company pays for financial education and financial planning programs. Only 24% said the cost of their programs was covered under a bundled 401(k) product. Nine percent offer expanded financial education or financial planning as an optional benefit paid for partially or fully by employees.

2. Capturing Management Buy-In

Just because you're sold on the idea that your employees need more financial education doesn't mean your senior management agrees. You probably won't get very far if you don't have the full support of the top brass. "It has to be high on their list of priorities to get them to spend money on it," says Avalone. He recently submitted a list of 25 recommendations to top management that were generated by a company-wide survey on employee quality-of-life issues. The recommendations include an expanded financial education program, a credit union with an ATM machine on the company's premises and some type of emergency back-up child care program.

Getting senior management buy-in usually requires a heavy sales campaign. You need to present solid reasons for launching a program and detailed explanations of cost, curriculum and the ultimate benefits. Of course, your sales pitch will be a lot easier if employee education is a major part of your company culture. No matter what the philosophy, however, the key to getting support, say most benefits managers, is timing. If business is in a downturn or you're expecting layoffs, you'll have to wait to approach the people at the top. One benefits manager at a major high-tech company says she's come up with detailed recommendations, but has put off approaching her bosses until business starts looking up. "It would be just stupid to do otherwise," she says.

Upper-level managers aren't the only ones who may need convincing. It may be the not so surprising little secret of benefits administration, but attitudes toward offering special programs tend to differ depending on which department does the overseeing. One administrator says she's had more success since educational programs were moved from the treasurer's office to human resources two years ago. "Before, the treasurer didn't understand why we needed to do more," she says. "Now, HR people want to know what we can do to serve the employee better."

3. Deciding Whom to Invite and When To Start

Once you have management buy-in, you'll have to decide whether or not to include spouses. Some benefits administrators feel strongly about inviting spouses along to make sure they're as informed as possible since most major family financial matters are decided by husbands and wives together. Others aren't so sure it's the company's job to educate the whole family. Scheduling classes at a family-friendly evening hour, however, doesn't necessarily guarantee high participation, as Dayton Hudson's experience shows.

An equally tricky problem is whether or not to hold the classes during work hours, particularly if it means interrupting production schedules. "Do you pull people off the manufacturing floor or get them to stay late?" asks Apple's Brewster. She thinks programs need to be run on company time in order to attract a big turn-out. But when? "If we wait too long, people are so tired they practically fall asleep," she says. Her solution is to schedule classes at the start of a shift—but during a quieter part of the quarter.

4. Meeting the Needs of a Diverse Employee Population

Acme's Brown is typical of many benefits administrators who struggle with the dilemma of educating a diverse group of employees. "We have people who don't know what a bond fund is and others who are actively trading in options," he says.

One solution is to run different programs that are aimed clearly at specific levels of financial sophistication. One session could focus on how the stock market works, another on futures trading; this helps employees choose the appropriate meeting to attend. It is important to let employees know how advanced the material will be at the beginning of the session so they don't lose interest if some of the information is either too complicated or too simple for them. At Montell, instructors began their sessions by explaining that some of the material might seem very basic to more money-savvy attendees, but because participants had different levels of knowledge, such information was necessary to get everyone up to speed. "Once they heard that, people said, okay, we understand, that's fine," says St. Clair.

DOWN THE ROAD

Broadening financial education for employees is uncharted terrain. No one knows to what degree it will become the norm, but one thing is certain: several pioneering companies are grappling with these major issues now, leading the way for the rest of the 401(k) community. Their experiences, strategies and insights can teach all plan sponsors valuable lessons about what your company's role in total financial education should be and how to go about shaping responsible, prudent and effective programs that boost bottom-line employee productivity.

The Editors of Investors Press

C H A P T E R
ONE

THE CUSTOMER SATISFACTION STRATEGY: FINANCIAL EDUCATION AT GTE

J. Randall MacDonald, Senior Vice President—
Human Resources and Administration
GTE Corporation

W hen is a financial education program also a customer satisfaction strategy? For GTE Corp. the answer is simple: when the financial education program helps employees cope with the major life events that we all face.

With $20 billion in revenues, GTE is one of the world's largest publicly held telecommunication companies. It provides local telephone and cellular phone service to millions. A primary goal of the financial education program we offer our 85,000 U.S. employees is to encourage commitment, loyalty and a sense of pride in the company by letting them know that GTE cares about them and their families. When our employees feel good about their jobs, we believe they are more productive and project better attitudes—which leads to more satisfied customers.

Our financial education program, perhaps the most extensive offered by any major U.S. corporation, received recognition from U.S. Secretary of Education, Richard Riley, when he said, "GTE's partnership with parents and children is a model we need to see in every single company. GTE is showing great leadership."

It's not surprising that a telecommunications company would use live satellite links to beam seminars on college planning, financial planning and career planning to a diverse employee population across the country. But our program would work even without high-tech delivery because it focuses on reducing stress by helping employees learn to manage and plan for major events in their personal and professional lives.

A FORMULA FOR SUCCESS: MORE EDUCATION EQUALS LESS STRESS

We live in stressful times. Our employees, like employees everywhere, feel stress at work and at home. Our objective is to take the edge off their stress by providing financial education that gives them the financial tools and knowledge they need to make more informed decisions about key life issues.

Too often, employees tend to fly by the seat of the pants in making decisions about important financial matters. No one likes to think about uncomfortable issues—estate planning and wills, for example—even though we all know we have to be prepared for the inevitable. By offering financial education geared to these common life events, we can make it easier for our diverse employee population to think ahead and manage these important issues more successfully.

Frankly, we were also concerned about the dramatic growth in 401(k) savings and the possibility that our employees may be relying solely on what they perceive as large account balances. Fifteen years ago, when 401(k) plans started, the savings numbers looked rather small. After almost two decades, however, 401(k) savings now represent a sizable part of the nest egg of a vast majority of our employees. We believe that employees need to understand how to balance their 401(k) savings with company retirement benefits, personal savings and other investments in an overall portfolio designed to provide for their long-term financial security.

We did not start out with the idea of offering a comprehensive financial education program. The program took shape in stages. First, through conversations with employees at all levels, our human resources department identified a need to help employees plan for their children's college education. We decided this was a very appropriate idea to pursue for 1995. Then, in response to the questions and issues raised at that initial college planning seminar, we realized that beginning in 1996 we needed to go further to help employees plan for other life events.

"COLLEGE PLANNING 101"

After making the decision to conduct a seminar on the ABCs of college planning, we had to determine exactly what to cover and who should present the information. As parents of college-bound students know, there is considerably more to college planning than filling out application forms. At a minimum, we had to cover the financial aspects of preparing for college (for example, how to apply for financial aid and how to use GTE benefit plans to help finance college). We also decided to touch on non-financial topics that concern parents and students, such as SAT testing and on-campus interviews.

At this point, we knew what would be covered in a seminar but still didn't know who would deliver the information. We looked first for in-house experts who were knowledgeable about specific topics, such as using GTE benefits as part of an overall plan to finance college. Then we searched for outside experts who were knowledgeable about the remaining topics to be presented. This strategy of enhancing internal expertise with external expertise is one we would repeat in our later education efforts.

The next problem was how to bring this seminar to thousands of employees scattered over a wide geographic area. Given our company's technology orientation, it was natural to solve the problem by arranging a teleconference using GTE's internal Business Television Network. We decided to cluster our speakers with live audiences at four sites and use satellite links to beam a full day of presentations, including questions and answers, to other GTE locations that wanted to receive the broadcast.

That first college planning seminar was highly successful, drawing more than 1,400 families (employees, spouses and high school-age children) at 18 sites around the country. The total cost was only about $80,000, which we think is amazingly low to reach such a large number of employees in so many locations. More important, however, was the very positive feedback we received through evaluation forms, notes and calls from employees.

As an example, Malinda Polite, a GTE administrative assistant who attended with her college-bound daughter, said: "The seminar showed me the company is concerned about employees and their families, not only on the job but off the job as well." Response was so enthusiastic that we repeated the seminar in 1996 with similar success.

PLANNING FOR OTHER LIFE EVENTS

As successful as the first college planning seminar was, we sensed that it wasn't enough. The questions our employees raised at this first seminar indicated they needed financial information that went beyond college financing. This realization sent us back to the drawing board; we analyzed the most important personal and professional events for which our employees required financial management skill.

We considered the critical events faced by employees at various stages of life, from those at age 21, who are just entering the workforce, to those at 70, who are living in retirement. Initially, the major life events we identified included: getting out of college and paying off student loans, getting married, buying a home, having children, educating them and planning for retirement.

This was a good start, but we also needed to get our employees' ideas about important life events they thought should be included in a financial educational program. We accomplished this by putting together a series of employee focus groups. A nearly universal complaint was not surprising: employees really didn't understand how the GTE pension plan worked and how the 401(k) plan was linked to it. We were surprised, however, at how interested employees were in having clear-cut information about wills, estate planning and taxes. Based on this input, we moved ahead to create a comprehensive financial planning seminar for 1996.

"FINANCIAL PLANNING 101"

As we had with the college planning seminar, we concentrated first on developing an agenda that would cover the information needed to build a successful long-term financial strategy. Our agenda expanded as we decided to include information about GTE benefits, retirement planning, financial goals, savings and investment basics, risk management issues, cash flow principles and estate and tax planning. We knew our internal experts could discuss compensation and benefits, but we needed to go outside for experts to cover the other topics.

We retained a professional financial education company to discuss cash flow, estate planning, insurance protection for assets, savings and investment strategies and retirement planning. Addressing the specific questions that were raised in the focus groups, we were careful to integrate a detailed discussion of how the GTE 401(k) fits into an overall strategy for retirement planning. Our 401(k) provider also participated, explaining how to obtain 401(k) account balances, make transfers and handle other transactions, and we had an insurance company present an overview of long-term care insurance.

THIS IS NO TIME
FOR YOUR EMPLOYEES
TO BE SITTING AROUND.

Regardless of who they are or where they are in their careers, it's none too early for your employees to be thinking about their long-term financial security.

- That's why every defined contribution retirement program from Allmerica Financial includes an integrated communication campaign. Worksite promotions, financial management seminars, complete enrollment kits, participant newsletters and toll-free telephone assistance provide all the information participants need to make the most of your plan. And provide a better understanding of what personal financial management is all about.

Defined Contribution Plans

As your employees advance along the learning curve, they'll retain their appreciation for your retirement plan. Allmerica Financial's model lifestyle portfolios can boost the confidence of even the least experienced investor. For those with a bit more market savvy, there's the appeal of funds from Fidelity, Janus, Nicholas-Applegate, Putnam Investments, Rowe Price-Fleming and other carefully selected money managers.

For details on our full-service 401(k), our other defined contribution plans or our complete portfolio of financial solutions for the worksite, call Allmerica Financial at 1-800-853-AFIS.

ALLMERICA
FINANCIAL®

ALLMERICA FINANCIAL INSTITUTIONAL SERVICES

On Screen/In Person/In Print/By Telephone

As with the college planning seminar, we wanted to reach as many employees and their spouses as possible with a single, all-day financial planning event. To accommodate the maximum number of attendees, we decided to hold this one-day seminar on a Saturday. Once more, the answer to how to do it came from our technology people, who arranged a teleconference to beam the seminar proceedings to 77 GTE sites throughout the country—a huge number of sites for an employee teleconference.

Although a teleconference is a great way to get a message to thousands of employees simultaneously, we faced the problem of bridging the time differences that separate many of our sites. If we started first thing in the morning on the East Coast, we would have to ask the West Coast people to show up unusually early; if we delayed the start until the mid-morning hours on the West Coast, the East Coast people would have to stay well past dinner. Our solution was to schedule the teleconference on core topics from 11 a.m. to 5:30 p.m. EST.

We used publicity to get the word out about the teleconference, including a series of printed employee bulletins, but were careful not to encourage attendance excessively. We knew there was pent-up demand and we wanted to be sure we could accommodate all who wanted to attend. When participants arrived at each location, they received a seminar binder with detailed information about company benefits, a workbook titled *Investing In Your Future* for hands-on use during and after the seminar, contact names and phone numbers for experts at GTE and outside, and copies of overheads reflecting the main ideas in each speaker's presentation.

The workbook, published by the financial education company, covered a wide variety of topics suited to the demographics of our employee population, including the basics of financial planning, goal-setting, cash flow planning, tax planning, investment management, risk protection, estate planning, college funding, Social Security contributions and benefits, health care coverage, career planning and financial resource management. Literally page by page, our experts took attendees through the seminar binder, covering the equivalent of perhaps several thousand dollars' worth of financial planning guidance during the day. We showed participants how to fill out the forms and complete the self-tests based on their individual financial situations, giving them the tools they needed to complete the planning process on their own and translate their plans into action long after the seminar was over.

Employees were told that outside experts were involved in the seminar; we highlighted our experts' professional and educational backgrounds in the promotion materials and in the binder. To avoid any potential liability, we were careful to position this seminar as an educational opportunity, stressing that the purpose was not to offer advice but to help employees create and manage their own financial plans for today and tomorrow. Although we arranged group discounts for employees who wished to use those suppliers' services, we did not endorse any specific suppliers. Because we realized that questions might come up later, we paid one of the suppliers to maintain a telephone hot line so that employees could continue to get their questions answered during the month following the seminar.

"Wish We Had More"

The first teleconferenced financial planning seminar drew over 4,000 employees and spouses. We had to do a bit of juggling to accommodate some attendees: when reservations for one of our Tampa, Florida sites exceeded the seating capacity, we shifted people to another GTE location in the area. During and after the seminar, we heard lots of positive comments, but we didn't just rely on verbal feedback.

We asked employees to fill out the evaluation forms inside the binders with comments on the quality of the content, the presenters, the information handouts, the time allotted to each topic and the conditions under which they viewed the broadcast. People were very willing to fill out the forms because they realized that their reactions and ideas would help us improve future programs.

Overall, employees were extremely pleased with the experience. We received letter after letter with testimonials from employees and spouses thanking us for putting on such a program. The biggest complaint—if it is a complaint—came from employees who said, "We wish we had more of this kind of education. Can we do it once a quarter or take even more time to cover these topics?"

The cost was just $150,000 to reach 4,000 families. In reality, however, when we count the "word of mouth" effect, including many people who have begun thinking about their financial strategies and plan to attend future GTE education programs, we know we reached thousands more.

What GTE Learned

Despite our success with both the college and financial planning seminars, we know there is room for improvement. Considering the feedback we received, it appears we had the right content for both seminars. However, we learned that some topics are less compelling than others, so we have to continue to invent ways to spice things up and keep the audience's attention.

This was a particular concern for the college planning seminar, where teenagers attended along with their parents. Although completing a financial aid application is of great interest to parents, teens may find such a topic tough to sit through. As a result, when we repeated this seminar, we changed the amount of time allocated to certain topics. Just as important, we added more tools for participants to use, such as mocked-up samples of good college applications. This enhanced the "hands-on" aspect of the seminar, making it even more useful to participants.

Employees also alerted us to the need to pay closer attention to presenters' on-camera skills. We chose our presenters for their expertise on specific topics, but that didn't mean all had polished on-camera skills. As a result, we're now providing TV training so presenters can communicate as effectively as possible using the teleconference medium.

Finally, we learned that for a financial education program to have real value for employees, it's important not to skimp or cut corners. This program is a unique opportunity to demonstrate that GTE cares about its employees and their families. We are committed to doing it right, giving employees the financial tools and information they need to manage their personal and professional lives successfully.

MORE EDUCATION FOR MORE LIFE EVENTS

Even though our financial education effort has been successful by any measure, we're not inclined to sit back and applaud ourselves. We continue to think about the key life events that affect every employee's financial situation and have selected career management as the logical next step in our financial education efforts.

GTE's first Career Management Seminar, to be held in 1997, will focus on how to manage a career from beginning to end. As with our other seminars, the purpose is to give employees the tools and knowledge they need to make informed decisions about their professional and personal lives.

Still, what works today won't necessarily work tomorrow. As we continue our education initiatives, we reevaluate our employees' educational needs every year and guard against overselling the seminars. In financial planning, for example, we have offered essentially the same content year after year, so we may decide to skip that seminar in 1998 but offer it again in 1999. We may change some of the life events and information to reflect the demographic needs of our ever-changing employee population. Although we can't easily foresee the exact direction our education program will take down the road, we can say with absolute assurance that it will continue to be linked to the events that can, and should, make a positive difference in our employees' personal and professional lives.

 SMART PILLS

➤ Whatever you decide to do, do it right. Don't skimp: give your employees the best and you'll be rewarded with higher productivity, more loyalty and better customer service.

➤ Use financial education to help employees plan for major life events that typically trigger the need for financial planning and resource management.

➤ For teleconferencing seminars, be sure presenters' skills are polished and appropriate to the media.

➤ Be prepared to answer employees' questions after a seminar or teleconference ends. If necessary, hire an outside company to field questions via a telephone hot line for a limited period of time.

➤ Adjust your financial education program periodically to reflect the needs of your changing workforce.

➤ Tap internal experts to teach employees about company benefits and look for knowledgeable external experts to present information on broader financial education topics.

FINANCIAL EDUCATION IN BITS AND BYTES

Dianne Nalin, Project Leader, Personal Financial Planning
Mark D. Harf, Project Leader, IBM 401(k) Program
IBM Corporation

Breaking new ground in financial education as well as in technology is all in a day's work for IBM. As a high-tech company approaching $80 billion in worldwide sales, with 120,000 employees eligible for the 401(k) plan, it is natural for us to apply cutting-edge electronic delivery of financial information to our employees. But our use of technology is only half the story: we know that employees need different financial information at different points in their lives and careers, so we use an ever-expanding range of messages and media to reach them whenever and wherever they are ready to learn about financial management.

IBM provides employees with up-to-the-minute, customized information and tools for personal financial management. With a click of the mouse, employees can read bites of information about financial education on our internal electronic bulletin board, put their own data into a unique interactive retirement planning model and get back personalized reports, and view 401(k) fund information and transactions on an Intranet site—complete with hyperlinks to external sources of information about financial planning for lifelong security. Non-electronic offerings include group workshops on a variety of financial planning topics, individualized financial planning analyses and employee newsletters covering 401(k) and investment topics.

This diverse menu of financial education options, among the most comprehensive offered by any company, allows our employees to pick and choose the specific information and format that meet their individual needs at any given time. Although many of our financial education options are technology-based, the underlying concept is not high-tech: we want to help our employees actively manage their personal finances and view financial education as more than a one-shot activity. By communicating many messages in a variety of media, we reinforce the importance of constantly learning and applying financial management principles to plan more effectively for a secure financial future.

Expanding The Financial Education Menu

For many years, IBM offered pre-retirement financial education to employees who were within five years of retirement. In intensive sessions spanning two or three days, employees learned about a variety of topics, including company retirement benefits, lifestyle changes and estate planning.

With the introduction of the 401(k) plan in 1983, our financial education program expanded to include comprehensive information about the size and growth of each employee's plan assets and how to manage investments. Despite the strong, positive feedback about these financial education programs, there was clearly an interest in and need for more information. In surveys, notes and personal conversations, many employees indicated that they would have benefited from access to retirement planning and financial management information earlier in their careers. By 1992, we were thinking about how to broaden the financial education menu to cover financial planning basics, as well as particular issues, such as tax planning.

Corporate culture also played a role in our decision to expand beyond pre-retirement and 401(k) education. More than ever before, IBM was putting a premium on personal responsibility and stressing a closer partnership on this topic with employees. Beefing up our financial education program was a concrete way to supplement our company benefits package and demonstrate even further our commitment to our employee partners. Our aim was to provide the additional tools and information our employees needed to take control of their individual financial situations. We wanted to help employees understand and use their benefits and feel equipped to actively manage their finances to achieve both short and long-term goals.

Senior management was attuned to the increasing importance of personal responsibility. They knew about the feedback from the pre-retirement education sessions and readily agreed that the time was right for expanding the financial education program. With their go-ahead, we tackled the challenge of making more general information available to all our employees.

We decided that employees could get a solid introduction to the overall principles of financial planning and to techniques for handling specific issues by attending group workshops. For employees who were interested in more personalized help, we decided to offer individual consultations and written financial plans. Although we now had a good idea of what the expanded financial education program should look like, we didn't know who would deliver it or how.

Outsourcing For Expertise

IBM does not have in-house resources dedicated to meet financial planning needs, so from the outset we knew that our program would have to be outsourced. Instead of working with a single outside provider as most companies do, we decided to contract with two outside providers. The purpose of this unusual arrangement was to give our employees choice and flexibility, allowing them to evaluate each provider's offerings on their own and then decide whether to work with one, or even both.

Our search for providers kicked off in late 1992, led by a team from our human resources department and our procurement organization, who worked with an out-

American Century Investments

P.O. Box 419385

Kansas City, MO 64141-6385

www.americancentury.com

IS THIS WHAT YOUR PLAN PROVIDER IS SERVING YOU?

At American Century, we know you have your own ideas about your retirement plan. That's why we don't bring you off-the-shelf solutions. We start by listening. Once we have a clear idea of the plan you want, we develop creative ways to make it happen. We're flexible in other ways, too. We offer a wide range of investments, including self-directed brokerage accounts with access to outside funds. And we happen to think that educating employees about the plan is *our* job, not yours. So we provide useful information to help them make better decisions. And to help make your job a little easier. So why settle for a generic plan? You can have exactly the plan you want from American Century. Call us today at: **1-800-988-9084.**

AMERICAN CENTURYsm

side consulting firm. The team sent a lengthy questionnaire to more than 50 financial services organizations, asking for information about their financial planning capabilities, fees and background on their organizational structure and personnel, including length of time in business, geographic coverage, financial education philosophy, and number and qualifications of the professionals who would deliver the services.

To ensure objectivity, our team reviewed each provider's questionnaire in a rigorous blind evaluation, scoring the answers on the basis of highly detailed criteria. We looked for providers with a proven track record in providing financial planning services, especially in the context of an employer-sponsored program. We also wanted our providers to be capable of bringing a quality education program to any IBM facility anywhere in the country, whether a major city or a rural setting. As a prerequisite to helping employees understand their total financial picture, our providers would have to acquire a working knowledge of IBM benefits. Using these criteria, we tallied up the scores and found that two providers came out well ahead of all the others.

We then negotiated contracts outlining the scope and cost of the financial education program. Although IBM does not pay the providers for running free group workshops for employees and their families, we arranged special rates for employees who request written assessments of personal financial data. To prevent the workshops from turning into sales pitches, the contract also prohibits the providers from soliciting IBM employees to buy additional products and services.

FINANCIAL EDUCATION A LA CARTE

By late 1993, we had final contracts and were ready to decide on the specific topics our providers would cover in group workshops during 1994 and beyond. Although our employees were interested in learning more about financial planning, we knew that many wanted a deeper knowledge of key topics related to their individual situations. To satisfy these needs, we had both providers offer a general financial planning workshop, as well as separate workshops on specialized topics such as managing investments, financing college, minimizing taxes, protecting income and assets and planning for retirement—each complete with hands-on workbooks and exercises.

Because our employees cannot properly plan their financial futures without taking into account their company benefits, we worked closely with both providers to customize the workshops to reflect IBM benefits and programs. To monitor quality, we carefully review outlines of every workshop, spot-check presenters at selected workshops and review the satisfaction surveys completed by employees who attend each workshop.

Most workshops are held on-site at IBM during work hours and on weekends to make it as convenient as possible for employees and family members to attend. From 1994 through November 1996, over 21,000 employees have attended these workshops and feedback from surveys and other sources shows that employees find them extremely valuable.

In addition to attending workshops, employees can have initial individual consultations and fill out a detailed questionnaire requesting a written personal financial analysis that considers IBM benefits and helps employees clarify their short and long-term financial goals and plans. The cost varies according to the level of detail included in the analysis. To date, over 18,000 employees have had written plans prepared. What makes this option especially appealing is the availability of reimbursement under IBM's Life Planning Account. This taxable reimbursement account provides employees with up to $250 annually to help cover outlays related to written analyses from the two providers, long-term care insurance or health education and fitness.

INFORMATION ONLINE

Although many employees have taken advantage of the workshops and written analyses, they also enjoy access to online delivery of financial information. We responded to this preference by offering several online sources of financial information. We post notices about the 401(k) plan and general financial planning on an internal IBM electronic bulletin board and encourage employees to check regularly to see what's new and what's changed. With this communication tool, we can target specific employee concerns and link financial planning to everyday events. In January, for example, we might suggest including financial planning among the employee's New Year's resolutions, while in March we might remind employees that tax time is an appropriate time to start financial planning. Because the bulletin board includes a feedback key, employees can quickly and easily e-mail a question or a comment to be researched and answered by experts in our National Human Resource Service Center.

One of our most widely used online tools is ESTIMATR, an internally managed retirement planning model that enables employees to input personal data and receive, just hours later, a customized report projecting the future value of their 401(k), pension and other savings at retirement. This tool not only helps employees spot gaps in their retirement planning in time to adjust their savings rate or investment mix, it allows them to look ahead to the actual future value of their own benefits and assess the rate of return they need to meet their desired income replacement level.

Accessible online to IBM employees since the late 1980s, and constantly upgraded and enhanced, ESTIMATR is a huge success. We received 220,000 report requests during 1995 alone and believe these reports are truly eye-openers for our employees. Seeing the exact value of their own benefits at retirement and the exact dollar amount of savings needed to supplement their benefits to ensure financial security brings the financial planning process vividly to life. Employees who have questions or comments about their ESTIMATR reports can call the National Human Resource Service Center toll-free, which adds a one-on-one dimension to this online tool.

Our newest online option is an Intranet Web site, which went live in May 1996 and received over 50,000 hits from employees in its first five months. By harnessing Web technology to offer financial education and 401(k) information, we can help employees become well-informed, confident investors who can better manage their 401(k) accounts. With a few keystrokes, employees can review 401(k) data, such as fund price updates, monthly investment results and loan rates. An upcoming enhancement will allow 401(k) account information to be downloaded into financial planning software tools such as Quicken Financial

Planner, enabling employees to do even more hands-on analysis and planning.

The site isn't limited only to 401(k) information: it also includes an expanding array of hyperlinks to selected articles from *Fortune, Money, Smart Money, The Wall Street Journal* and other respected publications. This approach puts employees in the driver's seat, allowing them to learn more about financial planning and other topics from sources outside IBM at their convenience. Because some questions are asked repeatedly, we will soon post a section of "Frequently Asked Questions". As with our other online tools, employee questions are e-mailed to the National Human Resources Service Center for research and response.

THE CROSSOVER EFFECT

Just because IBM has embraced technological delivery of financial information doesn't mean we've abandoned traditional print communications. Knowing that employees are receptive to different kinds of information at different times and in different formats, we have continued to produce a quarterly four-page newsletter for the 401(k) program. Despite the 401(k) focus, however, the content can certainly be applied to any financial planning situation because we cover portfolio diversification, how to maximize investment returns and other basic principles.

In fact, we have seen a definite crossover effect as employees take what they learn in one education vehicle and apply it in another context. We hear from many employees that the information in our newsletter helps them make non-401(k) mutual fund purchases and manage non-retirement investment portfolios. Our human resource experts say the questions they get are increasingly sophisticated and detailed, indicating that employees not only grasp the basics, they're actively searching for more information about how to manage their personal finances more competently.

Still, we must continue to reinforce the importance of financial planning, which is why we are always on the lookout for opportunities to deliver the message in a new way. Recently, for example, we included a brochure from ASEC, the American Savings Education Council, with a newsletter that talks about strategies and suggestions for long-term savings. The more we discuss the mechanics and the goals, the more we can demystify the financial planning process and motivate employees to take the first steps toward long-term financial security. We also communicate regularly with our small population of non-participants in the 401(k) plan, hoping to enroll them and encourage their saving for retirement.

RESULTS AND PLANS

Our innovative combination of interactive online tools, group workshops, professional financial analyses and newsletter delivery of financial information gets high marks from IBM employees. Surveys show that the education program consistently meets employee expectations. What's more, 401(k) portfolios are becoming increasingly diversified and our 401(k) participation rate has also grown substantially—signs that employees are putting into practice what they've learned. In 1993, the year before we implemented the financial education program, 46% of 401(k) assets were invested in GICs and 44% were in an equity fund. (The balance was in company stock, a balanced fund and bonds or cash.) As 1996 approached

Founders Balanced Fund made the short list of CIGNA, MetLife Defined Contribution Group, Hewitt Associates LLC, State Street Bank & Trust, and American Express Institutional Services.

But that's not the only reason it made

mine.

Obviously, when companies like these decided to offer our Balanced Fund in their defined contribution programs, we were pleased. Not many funds find themselves in such good company.

But that's not the only reason you should take a look. Consider Founders Balanced Fund's strong performance history. Its consistent investment style. And the fact that *The Wall Street Journal*, in its 1/13/97 issue, listed Founders Balanced Fund among the top performers, out of 271 balanced funds, for the 1-year period ended 12/31/96. If that's what it takes to get on your list, call Greg Contillo for a prospectus and more information on our Balanced Fund, or any of Founders' other no-load growth-and-income, international, growth, or aggressive growth funds.

Performance History:

Average annual total return as of 12/31/96

Founders Balanced Fund

1 year	5 year	10 year	20 year
18.76%	14.25%	12.42%	12.45%

★★★★ Morningstar Rating
The Fund received 4 stars among 1826, 1058, and 598 domestic equity funds for the 3-, 5-, and 10-year periods ended 12/31/96, respectively.

Founders Funds

Growth. Plain and Simple.

1-800-806-2986
www.founders.com

year-end, active plan participants had approximately 65% of their assets in equities, with 70% of new contributions going to equity allocations.

Since the debut of our comprehensive financial education effort in 1994, 401(k) participation has jumped from 80% to 91%, well above the industry average of 78%. This growth is due not only to education, but to an increase in matching contributions and our employee demographics. Our average employee is now about 40 years old with roughly 15 years of service. While many of our more tenured employees may have greater interest in financial planning issues than younger employees, our high 401(k) participation rate indicates that a good cross-section of our employee population maintains a strong interest.

Looking ahead, we will continue to expand our financial education menu and reach out to different segments of our employee population. Given our high-tech orientation, we will improve our Intranet site and other online tools to provide even more access to timely information about 401(k) accounts and financial planning. Another way we're reaching out is by promoting the financial planning options in the new-hire packages we provide to employees when they join the company. Whatever media we use, we plan to pursue the importance of financial planning to ensure that our employees remain actively involved in working toward their secure financial future.

 S M A R T   P I L L S

➤ If you offer online financial information, be staffed and ready to research and respond promptly to questions from employees.

➤ Consider using more than one provider to offer employees choice and flexibility in financial planning services.

➤ Communicate! Communicate! Communicate! Because employees are open to learning about different topics at different times, use a variety of media to deliver the financial education message and enhance the crossover effect.

➤ Stimulate interest among new employees by promoting your financial education program in materials they receive when they are hired.

CHAPTER THREE

Financial Education: Up Close And Personal

Evon E. Beland
Manager, Benefits and Administrative Systems
Millipore Corporation

Start with basic investment concepts, season with a personal touch and add a twist of technology—that's Millipore's recipe for financial education success. A $600 million multinational maker of purification products for microelectronics production, analytical laboratories and biopharmaceutical manufacturing, Millipore has put financial education on the front burner. Our goal is to keep cooking up programs that empower our 1,500 employees in the U.S. and 3,350 employees worldwide to manage their careers, financial responsibilities and personal lives more effectively.

Our "work/life programs" are designed to help employees maintain a healthy balance between their professional and personal responsibilities. We offer partially paid family care leave, flextime scheduling and sabbatical leave as part of programs that enable employees to better manage their work and home life. The company's integrated approach to employee benefits was recently recognized by *Working Mother* magazine, which named Millipore to its 1996 list of the 100 most family-friendly U.S. companies.

Millipore sees financial education as a natural extension of our work/life programs. Sparked by employee diversity, changes in 401(k) investment options and a desire to help motivate employees to plan for their future, we have devised a number of solutions to meet the challenge of educating employees about financial matters. Over time, our approach to financial education has become more high-tech/high-touch, having evolved from group workshops covering basic financial concepts in 1995 and personal financial counseling in 1996 to Intranet-based, personalized financial communication planned for 1997.

Because few companies offer access to one-on-one financial counseling through open enrollment in flex benefits, we had no models to follow when we began our program. Similarly, we are among the first companies to plan personal home pages on the Intranet so that employees can check benefits and run financial models at any convenient time. Finding our way through the maze of education possibilities has been made a little easier by our insistence on personalization, the essential ingredient featured in all our programs. We provide financial education that helps employees apply the information and tools we give them to their individual needs and situations.

NEW INVESTMENT OPTIONS, NEW ATTITUDES TOWARD RISK

Despite our longtime dedication to work/life programs, we did not consider financial education until fairly recently. Traditionally, Millipore had a paternalistic attitude toward its employees, offering only conservative investment options for 401(k) participants.

Over time, however, we realized that our employee population was becoming more diverse: they had varying levels of financial savvy, different appetites for risk and increasingly asked for more aggressive investment options. In response, management decided to add five new investment options in 1995, including an S&P index fund, a balanced fund, an aggressive growth fund, an international fund and a guaranteed income fund. At the same time, Millipore decided it had a responsibility to demonstrate a sense of partnership with our employees by providing a more fundamental financial education that would help them make more informed choices about 401(k) investments and retirement planning.

Legally, we could have limited our education program to 401(k) planning and investment issues. But in the current business environment where no one is guaranteed a job for life, we were committed to going beyond legal requirements such as 404(c) regulations. As part of our dedication to employee empowerment, we realized that it is necessary to help all employees manage their own careers and personal finances more effectively, regardless of their job or income level or length of service. The company was already providing top executives with financial planning services; we decided to build on this program, making such knowledge and expert assistance available and affordable to all employees.

We faced a particular challenge in encouraging younger employees to begin their retirement planning early in their careers. These employees needed to know that it would be much more difficult for them to start building adequate funds for a secure future when they were only five or even ten years away from retirement. Of course, those who participated in Millipore's 401(k) plan were already taking their first steps toward retirement planning. Now we wanted to help all employees get a faster start and step up the pace of planning for their future financial security.

LEARNING ON COMPANY TIME

Our financial education program debuted in early 1995—at the same time we introduced the five new 401(k) investment options—with a series of group workshops at Millipore locations around the country. Because I have only one staff member who devotes three-quarters of her time to 401(k) activities, handling all transfers as well as accounting and financial reporting, we were not prepared to launch the workshops on our own. Clearly, I needed outside help.

Outsourcing the workshops to tap the expertise of an experienced financial education supplier led us to the company that serves as recordkeeper and actuary for our defined benefit and defined contribution plans. It has an in-depth knowledge of our retirement programs and enjoys an excellent reputation for financial

When it Comes to Employee Education, We're in a Class by Ourselves

Effective Ongoing 401(k) Education at Pillsbury

The biggest challenge in ongoing retirement plan education is breaking through the daily "noise" to get key messages to employees.

Pillsbury focus groups indicated employees didn't always have a clear picture of the role their 401(k) plan played in their retirement benefit package. To differentiate the plan, we introduced a campaign that used humorous and thought-provoking images of the word "401(k)." The campaign presented basic information in small, frequent doses over a six month period. Over time, it served to redefine perceptions of the plan for employees, giving it its own identity as a 401(k) and helping to increase plan participation.

Helping ShopKo Employees Understand Diversification

Asset diversification was a key goal for ShopKo Stores, Inc., with participants often limiting themselves to the income and equity options of their plan.

An education campaign called, "You've Got The Power," helped show employees how they could take control of their investment choices through increased diversification.

The campaign proved to be successful as empowered participants diversified their assets across all investment choices.

Every 401(k) plan presents its own unique challenges for employee education. American Express Institutional Services has gone to the head of the class by helping companies provide employees with the information they need to help them successfully meet their goals.

From building awareness of the plan to measuring program effectiveness, American Express Institutional Services provides a comprehensive, disciplined approach to educating your employees. To find out more, call Ward Armstrong at 1-800-437-0600.

Institutional Services

planning education. We teamed with this supplier to develop the format and content for a free two-hour workshop called "Planning Your Financial Future". For this first round of financial education, our goal was to present basic investment concepts, explain the fundamentals of how to save for retirement and emphasize the magic of compounding investment returns over time.

Next, we faced the challenge of delivering our message to as many employees as possible. To encourage widespread attendance and stress the importance of the subject matter, we offered those first workshops on company time, rather than at lunch or after work, and made it even easier for our employees to attend by holding the workshops either at a company site or in the field. Our sales force, for example, attended their workshops during the annual sales conference at an off-site location.

As important as the workshops were, however, we did not want them to disrupt our daily operations. To avoid conflicts, we worked closely with departmental supervisors to determine the best time and day for their employees to attend a workshop. Once the schedule was set, every employee, including top managers, received a personal invitation to attend a workshop at a particular time; we offered 44 workshops in all. Using a variety of internal communications, such as the company newsletter, we heralded the value of the workshops and prepared employees for learning about financial planning.

Top management fully supported this educational effort. In fact, our CEO received the same personal invitation as every other employee and he attended his workshop when assigned, as did the Vice President of Human Resources and other senior managers. The attendance of all our executives was a powerful and valuable example for the other employees.

HOLD MY HAND!

Our workshops were a big hit. More than 90% of our U.S. employees attended and 99.7% of those surveyed said that they would recommend the workshops to others. Equally important, overall participation in the 401(k) increased from 73% to 84% during the two quarters following the workshops and we saw a 25% reduction in fixed-income funds with a shift to more diversified portfolios; by the end of the first quarter following the workshops, the ratio of investments in the fixed-income funds had dropped from 40% to 31% as employees moved more of their money into equity funds. This shift indicated that employees were putting into practice what they had learned about planning for a more secure future.

Although the workshops were a good start, many employees said they wanted even more help. Some confided that they were carrying considerable debt. Some described other financial situations that were difficult to manage, such as saving for retirement while juggling mortgage, education or child care expenses. On the same day, one employee making $25,000 and another making $100,000 told me that although they recognized the need to save, they didn't even know how to start. "I understood what the financial planners said," one explained, "but I need somebody to hold my hand and give me more personalized counseling about how to apply the concepts to my own situation." The message was loud and clear: employees needed a more personalized approach to help them put theory into practice.

"So anyway, I told my broker, buy 500 shares immediately of Smith Semiconductor. I made a 50% profit in two days, pulled out and then got into this venture capital deal in China…"

"OK, let's see, 15%…Well, 10% would be…Hmmm…8 plus 5 is 13… carry the one…"

SELECTING A FINANCIAL PLANNING SUPPLIER

We decided that offering one-on-one financial counseling would personalize the information employees received in the workshops. There was no need to reinvent the wheel, however; we already had a proven and successful financial planning program for our executives. For many years, Millipore, like many employers, retained an outside financial counseling company to provide top executives with sophisticated financial planning and tax services. Because this company had already established its credibility with us, we knew that top management would be more comfortable with the idea of allowing it to make similar services available on a voluntary basis to our entire employee population.

This company did not sell any investment products—another important point in its favor. As it turned out, our timing was excellent. The company was in the process of developing a plan to offer individual financial counseling services to employees and it was eager to join us in testing a personalized program for ours. Together, we planned a pilot program to start in the fall of 1995, during Millipore's first company-wide open enrollment for flex benefits.

PILOTING AFFORDABLE PERSONALIZED COUNSELING

Because this was the first time we were offering all employees personalized financial planning services, we decided to test employee reaction to a variety of programs: tax preparation, estate planning and two options for financial planning (development of a personalized plan with or without individualized counseling). Knowing that ongoing personal contact was important to our employees, our supplier agreed that any employee who signed up for one or more services could also call a special hot line number to discuss issues related to the financial questionnaire they had to complete prior to meeting with a counselor.

As we prepared to launch the pilot, we were concerned about attendance and cost. There was no way to project how many employees might take advantage of the new services. Even after employees enrolled, they didn't have to call for appointments until they were ready to sit down with a counselor. This meant that our supplier couldn't anticipate or prepare in advance for the volume and timing of the employee response.

Cost was also a big issue. If employees thought the cost was too high, they wouldn't participate. We knew we had to negotiate a reduced group rate to encourage employees to sign up for these personalized services. Before negotiating price with the supplier, we talked with employees who had asked for personalized services to find out how much they would be willing to pay. We were able to agree on a relatively low cost structure for the first year to jump start the program and gauge employee interest. This also gave the financial planning company a chance to see if it could offer personalized services profitably through such a program.

Our group rates allowed employees to purchase each of the four services for a flat fee. The most expensive was comprehensive financial counseling with a personalized plan, which cost $350. Because this was still a sizable outlay for many employees, we looked for a way to make paying for the services both affordable and convenient. The answer was to allow employees to pay for the services in one of two ways: by applying flex credits or by after-tax payroll deductions spread throughout the year. These arrangements encouraged employees to use the services by allowing them to avoid additional out-of-pocket costs and lump-sum payments.

Despite the personalized nature of the services, Millipore's costs were minimal. Occasionally, employees left after receiving their financial counseling but before completing all the payroll deductions for services. We put a system in place to recover any unpaid balance in these rare cases. There were also some administrative costs associated with operating the program, but we accepted these as part of our responsibility to educate our employees.

Once we had arranged for the services, we had to motivate employees to sign up. The message we delivered was that personal financial planning would provide valuable information about managing investments and creating individual financial strategies. We announced the pilot program in our employee newsletter and in the flex benefits open enrollment booklet distributed to every employee. We also allowed employees to sign up for financial planning services, among other flex benefits, using the in-house interactive voice response system we introduced in 1991 for 401(k) enrollments and transactions.

To address the issue of potential liability, these announcements stated clearly that Millipore did not recommend or endorse the financial planning company's advice. We used wording that carefully clarified the educational nature of the program, noting that the financial planners would "provide the information necessary for you to make a decision". We also reassured employees that the personal data they shared with counselors would be held in strict confidence.

LESSONS LEARNED

Although we had not set specific goals, we were pleased with the response to this pilot program: about 11% of eligible employees signed up for at least one of the services. Through an informal telephone survey, we learned that employees who

DIAGNOSTIC REPORTS

*How are our employees allocating their contributions? What is our participation rate? Do participants use the automated voice response system? How? The next time you want **answers to your questions**, you'll have the information you need.*

AUTO ENROLLMENT

*Signing up for a 401(k) plan should be easy, for both you and your employees. Scudder removes the endless paperwork from your desk. And, as your partner, we will **automatically inform** your new employees when they're eligible. They can even **enroll** by phone!*

Think beyond.

A 401(k) plan is crucial to your employee benefit package, but it shouldn't be a burden on your company. As your 401(k) partner, we would consider it our responsibility to make the plan as simple for you to administer as you would like. And we will gladly create a package of innovative services specific to your desired level of control. After all, that's what a partnership is all about—helping one another succeed. To explore how a partnership with Scudder can give you the right 401(k) plan for your company, please **call us at 1-800-323-6105, ext. 407.**

SCUDDER

DESKTOP PLAN MANAGER™

*You should be able to manage your 401(k) in any way that **works for you**. If you choose, you can instantly handle virtually every day-to-day operation from your personal computer. Our Desktop Plan Manager can make it easy.*

SCUDDER 401(k) PROGRAM

THINK TOGETHER

used the services were very pleased, evaluating the counselors as "first class" and "very professional". One employee who was on the verge of retirement said she was able to use what she learned during her counseling session to make more informed investment decisions about her distribution from Millipore's pension plan. Even with this enthusiastic response, feedback from the pilot indicated that we still had some fine tuning to do.

The pilot confirmed our intuition that our employees' needs differ according to their income levels. Families at higher income levels typically face more complex financial planning challenges than families at other income levels because of more complex portfolios of real estate, securities or other assets.

Unexpectedly, however, we learned that the relatively low cost of the personal financial planning service led to some misperceptions. Some higher-income employees questioned whether financial planning that cost only $350 could really be sophisticated enough for their families' needs. In fact, the financial planning company found that it wasn't able to make a profit delivering the most comprehensive services to higher-income employees for that flat fee, so the cost had to be increased for such services.

We were surprised that the financial plan preparation services generated the most administrative problems. Employees held off until the last minute because they had to spend time gathering documents and completing the supplier's questionnaire before the appointment. A few employees asked for more time because of changes in their work or personal schedules. Others complained that they were intimidated by the complex and lengthy questionnaire. Even after the supplier substituted a shorter, simpler questionnaire, we still had to prod employees to make appointments. Finally, with the year-end deadline fast approaching, we gave employees a firm deadline for sending in their paperwork. Our supplier was then inundated with requests for appointments and some employees had to wait.

Once we analyzed the results of the 1995 pilot, we moved ahead to find solutions to these problems and made plans to roll out an improved program in 1996.

TAILORING SERVICES TO VARIOUS INCOME LEVELS

We tackled the problem of how to provide services to employees at different income levels first. We varied the original formula by targeting three income levels for customized services: $40,000 or less, $40,000–$100,000 and over $100,000. Although estate planning was offered for $250 to employees at any income level as a separate option, all other offerings were tailored to the specific needs of families at each income level.

Starting with the 1996 program, employees at the lower income level can have a customized financial plan prepared for $250; for $350, they can have the customized financial plan and one hour of personal counseling. Employees with family incomes of $40,000–$100,000 can sign up for more comprehensive services: a customized financial plan and two one-hour sessions of personal counseling cost $650 (tax preparation services increase the cost to $950).

Employees with family incomes over $100,000 can select essentially the same services that are provided for our top executives. These employees may need debt structuring, risk management and other sophisticated services. They can have a financial plan developed and receive two 90-minute sessions of counseling for

$1,500; with tax preparation the cost goes to $2,000.

We devised two solutions to avoid the bottlenecks caused by employees who delay in making appointments for the counseling they have selected. The financial planning company reorganized its process in order to handle the increased workload at tax time and other peak periods. This change smoothed communication with employees during crunch periods and allowed the supplier to accommodate employees who call for appointments at the last minute. To facilitate the process, we now follow up with employees who sign up and pay for services but procrastinate about calling for appointments. We also measure the quality of these sessions by calling employees and asking if they were satisfied with the services they received.

STAYING AHEAD OF THE CURVE

We are constantly searching for ways to personalize our employee benefit programs even further and financial education is no exception. We will continue to offer group workshops and personalized financial planning services every year because feedback shows that they are well received—a tribute to the professionalism and expertise of our suppliers. But we're also looking at other ideas that will empower our employees and help them make better long-term financial decisions.

In 1997 we plan to develop an Intranet-based program of individual home pages for every employee. When the system is fully operational, employees will be able to go to their home pages and see up-to-date details about their personal benefits. We also want to give our employees the capability to do simple "what if" modeling that will help them consider specific alternatives for their personal financial plans and think through the impact of different decisions before they make any changes.

Our Intranet project is the next logical step in Millipore's commitment to improving our work/life programs. With this cyberspace initiative, we will enter a new era of high-tech/high-touch financial education that brings even more financial information up close and personal for every employee.

➤ Involve top management in the process of education and have them set an example for participation in your financial education program.

➤ Plan convenient schedules for financial education seminars to encourage greater participation and avoid conflict with employees' work duties.

➤ If you outsource financial education, set specific criteria for the supplier, such as not selling investment products.

➤ Be sure you and your supplier are prepared to handle higher demand during peak periods.

➤ For programs that carry a fee, set prices that reflect perceived value and cover the supplier's costs for delivering quality services.

➤ Monitor enrollment, usage of programs and employee satisfaction.

CHAPTER FOUR

PIONEERING LIFETIME FINANCIAL EDUCATION

Judy C. Underwood
Senior Retirement Advisor and Program Administrator
Philip Morris U.S.A.

A pioneer among companies offering financial education to employees on the brink of retirement, Philip Morris U.S.A., a division of the world-wide tobacco, food and beverage manufacturer, now helps all its employees plan for lifelong financial security from the very start of their careers.

More than 25 years ago, we offered classes to employees who were about to retire, explaining the range of company retirement benefits and the tax implications of distribution decisions. When our division added a 401(k) program in 1983 as part of the existing deferred profit-sharing plan, we expanded our benefits education effort to cover the mechanics and advantages of 401(k) participation. Our financial education program has continued to grow ever since—beyond retirement and benefits education to comprehensive information on investment strategies and personal financial planning for employees at all stages of their careers.

Although the company does not match any 401(k) contributions, our 15,000 eligible employees may receive as much as 15% of their annual salary in the deferred profit-sharing program, depending on the company's profitability. Retirement information and 401(k) education are still important, but we believe that in this era of corporate downsizing and early retirement, more financial education is essential. Philip Morris recognizes its responsibility to help employees become informed, self-confident savers and investors as they chart their lifelong financial course. To succeed, they need comprehensive financial education from the first day of their careers so they can manage their money for smooth sailing up to retirement and beyond.

We make a special effort to help all our employees integrate their 401(k) accounts and other company benefits into one cohesive financial strategy. Our new financial education program targets three specific employee groups and addresses a wide range of personal financial issues. For younger employees, the emphasis is on the basics of financial planning, with an eye toward developing long-term strategies. For employees who are closer to retirement, the emphasis is on estate planning and funding retirement. And for highly compensated executives, the emphasis is on covering the complex issues related to qualified and non-quali-fied retirement benefits.

RESPONDING TO CHANGING EDUCATIONAL NEEDS

Our decision to offer education for total financial security evolved, in part, as a response to trends in the American workplace. Like many other companies, Philip Morris was well aware that most employees often work for more than one company during the course of their careers, forcing them to juggle benefits from various sources and make decisions that affect their future security long before they retire.

We also knew that our employees did not have the skills or motivation to incorporate their Philip Morris benefits into long-term strategies for financial planning and saving. Our benefits administration staff, who meet individually with different employees every day, learned that many relied heavily on company benefits, unaware that these benefits alone may not be sufficient to fund a comfortable retirement. We became concerned about our employees' general lack of knowledge and began to lobby management for permission to offer basic financial education that would help employees maximize and supplement their benefits, handle investments and save enough money for a secure financial future.

Senior management supported the idea and we began to shape the content and format of our program. A planning group of human resource personnel from each division met to identify and discuss which key financial topics we needed to cover. Based on this group's firsthand experience with employees, we realized they needed understandable definitions of stocks, bonds and mutual funds as well as a working knowledge of asset allocation, diversification and market trends in order to manage their investments competently over time. We were also especially interested in helping younger employees get an early start on the financial planning process so they would be informed financial managers at every stage of their lives.

TARGETING THREE DISTINCT EMPLOYEE GROUPS

Recognizing that employees have different educational needs, we decided not to offer the same information to all employees. As we looked for ways to target our financial education efforts, we identified three distinct employee groups, each of which had specific needs and situations.

The first group included younger employees, who will probably work for more than one company during their careers. We wanted these employees to be able to move on with their lives in the event Philip Morris were to downsize in the future. Some had just joined the company; others had been with Philip Morris for a short time. All needed solid information about the basics of financial management, investing and long-term planning. How are long-term financial goals set? What can a young employee do today to start planning for retirement? What investment options are available and what are the tax implications of specific types of investments?

The second group included employees who were well into their careers and expected to retire from Philip Morris in ten to 15 years. We recognized that this group had different financial and educational needs from those of younger employees. Many had begun to accumulate savings and needed to go beyond the basics to learn about concepts such as diversification, risk and estate planning—a hot button among these longer-service employees.

The third group included highly compensated executives. They needed the same information as those in the two other groups, plus additional information on how to integrate qualified and non-qualified retirement benefits into their overall financial strategies. They also needed to understand the tax implications of various non-qualified benefits so they could protect their assets.

Identifying these three groups was a good start, but we still had to decide how, when and where to deliver the information. Rather than offer a lengthy one-shot workshop once a quarter, we decided on an ongoing series of 90-minute classes covering 12 topics for each group, including financial strategies, investment basics, asset allocation, retirement strategies and college planning. This format enabled us to present much more information and gave employees the chance to pick and choose those classes that met their personal needs.

We call the education program for younger employees "Career Financial Planning". Employees close to retirement attend a "Comprehensive Planning" workshop, while highly compensated executives focus on "Executive Retirement Planning". We offer all classes on-site at Philip Morris locations, scheduling them during the work day to make the education program easily accessible to all employees.

Outsourcing The New Program

At this point, we were faced with the problem of determining who would present the programs. Clearly, Philip Morris did not have the internal resources to develop and conduct an ongoing series of classes, nor did we have the in-house skills to conduct financial planning seminars for our employees. We also wanted to avoid the risk of giving "advice" to employees who attend the classes. As a result, we decided to outsource the education classes.

First, we set specific objectives to guide the process of evaluating potential suppliers, who had to be capable of providing solid educational information customized for our employees' needs. We would not allow the classes to be used as a forum to sell investment products or other services. The supplier had to be large enough to provide a consistent level of education to Philip Morris employees anywhere in the United States. Finally, we wanted the instructors to have the appropriate credentials, such as the CFP (Certified Financial Planner) certification.

Next, we asked a number of investment management firms, insurance companies and financial education specialists to submit detailed proposals on how they would meet our needs. We narrowed the field to a small group of companies who made presentations on the program content they could provide. The input from these companies helped shape and tailor the agendas we ultimately set for our classes.

After weighing each of the finalists' credentials and capabilities, we chose a single company to handle all the classes. The decision to use this company was based, in part, on the independent status of its financial consultants, who we believed could be more objective in offering advice. Equally important, we felt that our employees would have confidence in this company's professionalism and knowledge of financial strategies.

Next, we negotiated an agreement covering content, cost and legal issues. The company conducts the classes without charge; employees are made aware that the educators are not Philip Morris employees, but professional financial consultants. Employees can request a free, one-hour individual consultation and they

receive a 20% discount if they decide to work with the financial advisor on a personalized plan.

Monitoring Content And Presentation

With an instructor from an outside company leading the classes, we had some concerns about the way content would be presented. In particular, we wanted to be sure that any discussion of employee benefits was accurate and up-to-date, so we held a class to teach the educators about Philip Morris benefits. As an insurance policy, we decided to have one of our own benefits specialists present in every class, ready to clarify questions about Philip Morris benefits and monitor the presentation style and educational content.

Both the benefits specialist and the financial advisor begin every class with a verbal disclaimer reminding the audience that Philip Morris is not endorsing this particular company, presenter or any specific products. We tell employees that we are making this information available for educational purposes only, to help our employees make their own informed financial decisions.

Class Is In Session

We designed the classes to be interactive, with presentations tailored to the needs of each group followed by time for Q&A. To encourage our employees to attend, we run the program from January to June, suspend it in the summer months when many employees are on vacation and begin again in October. Although attendance was not mandatory, we expected interest to be high.

Because of the differences in employees' schedules, we decided to hold multiple classes—as many as five per day—at selected Philip Morris locations. Classes were scheduled immediately before and after work shifts, as well as during mid-day lunch periods. Employees who work in the manufacturing center, for example, can go to class before work, attend classes during staggered lunch hours or go to class

With Merrill Lynch, your 401(k) program may not look quite like any other. But it will fit you to perfection.

At Merrill Lynch, your 401(k) program can be tailored specifically to your unique requirements. We can help you develop solutions in the key areas of 401(k) program design:

Bundled Services

By bundling employee benefit and record-keeping services, you'll gain maximum flexibility and value from your plan.

Technology

Merrill Lynch has a flexible systems architecture. And we are committed to investing in state-of-the-art technology to best serve you and your employees.

Investment Management Expertise

Every client benefits from the firm's highly ranked investment management expertise and access to nearly 400 mutual funds.

Education and Communications

Merrill Lynch's award-winning education and communication programs, built upon our financial planning and investment expertise, are proven to increase plan participation.

For more information, call Donna Winn, First Vice President, at 609-282-2233. Because there's a big difference between your 401(k) planning needs and everybody else's.

The difference is Merrill Lynch.

A tradition of trust.

just after their shifts end. Spouses are invited to all classes, but we especially encourage their attendance at the Comprehensive Planning sessions for employees who will retire from Philip Morris in ten to 15 years.

Because we wanted to get the program up and running quickly, we had time to mount only a limited communication effort before classes began in January 1996: we posted notices on bulletin boards and announced the classes on the company's closed circuit television system, which can be viewed in company cafeterias.

Unfortunately, classes started during a blizzard, dampening the success of these early efforts. We were pleasantly surprised, however, at the number of employees who braved the weather to attend. Still, we quickly realized that we had to promote the program more aggressively if we were to attract more employees. After classes started, we mailed announcements to employees at home and described the program in company publications with details and the class schedule. This boosted attendance considerably. To avoid any communication gap before the next round of classes, we plan to launch a more concentrated communication effort to encourage attendance, including another home mailing with a more detailed list of topics.

PUSHING A HOT BUTTON

The level of attendance shows that our program has hit a hot button among employees. In the first six months, 1,030 employees and spouses—more than 8% of eligible employees—attended a total of 62 classes held in six different locations. Although we had hoped for higher attendance, we were off to a good start, considering that so many employees were working six or seven-day overtime schedules in the manufacturing areas.

With one year of financial education under our belt, we're actively soliciting employee feedback to help tailor the content and presentation of this year's classes. After each class, employees receive evaluation forms so they can suggest topics they want to learn about and rate the presenter, workbooks and content. We have learned that employees want more information about how to make the most of Philip Morris benefits and about specific topics such as asset allocation and college planning. In response, we have beefed up benefits coverage and added coverage where requested. When the instructors cover estate planning, for example, they now explain the tax consequences of assigning life insurance benefits to a trust so that the funds will not be included in the employee's estate.

Currently, we are concluding a survey to find out what attendees particularly enjoy about the classes, what else they need to know and how we can customize the program even further to fit their specific needs. Although the final results are not yet in, early responses confirm what we learned from the evaluation forms: most employees like the program very much. They gained valuable insights from it and want the classes to explain specific Philip Morris benefits.

ON THE HORIZON

Although our program is only a year old, we're already thinking of ways to keep it fresh and engaging for all employees. To sustain the interest of past attendees and attract new ones, we will offer two different topics in every two-month period.

One will repeat a topic covered in an earlier class for those employees who could not attend the first series of classes, while the other topic will be new.

Our financial education program has been so successful in terms of attendance and meeting employee needs that other divisions of Philip Morris are now looking at rolling out something similar. Because the benefits are nearly the same throughout the company, their programs might need only a few modifications to be relevant for their audiences.

Despite the success of the classroom-based program, however, we are exploring the use of other educational vehicles that can reach employee groups with specific information needs. Our first effort, geared toward employees who are about to retire, is a new video with details about retirement benefits, publicized through notices tacked onto company bulletin boards and announcements on our closed-circuit television system. This video supplements the information provided in the financial education classes and demonstrates how employees can optimize their Philip Morris benefits. It discusses key retirement-related issues, such as the tax implications of taking distributions, and explains ideas for providing survivor benefits for spouses without reducing the employees' retirement benefits. When employees schedule interviews prior to retirement, we send them the video to provide background information. However, other employees may also want to view the video to learn more about the benefits they can expect when they retire. Any employee can take the video home and view it with a spouse and/or a financial or tax planning professional.

A computer modeling program that allows employees to do their own retirement planning is in the very early planning stages. Some employees have requested such a program and although we have contacted a number of suppliers regarding availability, we have not yet committed to this new tool. We are not sure that enough of our employees have the skills and the access to a personal computer to make a modeling program viable. Even if the program were available on the local area network at Philip Morris locations, there are some employees who do not have access to the network system.

Legal issues are also a concern. What if some employees, using the program on their own, input incorrect data or misunderstand some of the information and make inappropriate decisions? We plan to revisit this project in the coming months to see how we might resolve these issues and offer a modeling tool that everyone can use productively.

On the horizon is a plan to post benefits information and financial education class schedules on an Intranet system. Whether we decide to use computer modeling, add more videos, modify our classes or distribute information via the Intranet, our ultimate goal remains consistent. Philip Morris is committed to offering all its employees, both young and old, the financial education they need to manage every phase of their lives. By helping our employees become more competent and confident in their personal financial management, we can set them on the path toward financial security long before and after retirement.

S M A R T   P I L L S

➤ Offer financial education to employees at all stages of their careers. Don't limit the education program to employees who are about to retire. Learn what financial information employees need to know and when they need to know it.

➤ Consider offering a series of workshops devoted to individual topics, rather than trying to cover everything in a single comprehensive workshop.

➤ Consider alternating classes on new and repeat topics to attract new attendees and sustain the interest of previous attendees.

➤ Integrate detailed information about your company's benefits into all financial education presentations to show employees how to maximize and supplement their benefits within their individual financial strategies.

CHAPTER FIVE

Back To Basics:
Educating A Diverse Employee Population

Jan Hill Bucheit, Manager, Benefit Communications
Mary Lee Crowley, Manager, Benefit Administration
Waste Management, Inc.

D ifferences in employee location, reading level, language and attitudes toward money are among the many complex issues and challenges Waste Management, Inc. faces in designing a financial education program for its employees. Few companies have an employee population as diverse and widely dispersed as ours, the world's leading waste management services company with $10.2 billion in sales.

Of 73,000 employees worldwide, 30,000 work at 1,100 U.S. sites and are eligible currently for our 401(k) plan. But these numbers don't begin to reveal the dramatic differences among our employees. Their job descriptions range from helpers on the backs of garbage trucks to executives in management offices. Education levels vary as widely as reading levels, the average of which is approximately eighth grade. We also face differences in language: 1,500, about 3% of our total U.S. employee population, are Spanish-speaking.

Varying attitudes toward financial education are another challenge. Many employees who participate in our 401(k) plan are eager for more education about long-term savings and investment options. Non-participants, however, are generally suspicious about putting their money in a 401(k) and tend to be less knowledgeable about company benefits and financial management.

Confronted by this diversity in attitudes and information, we realized that Waste Management had to go back to basics to provide financial education, moving beyond reading materials to offer information in ways that would be comfortable for each employee. Our solution is to plan a financial education program that blends videos, workbooks, live and televised seminars, personal counseling and telephone access to the 401(k) plan provider for answers to specific employee questions.

BOOSTING PARTICIPATION, REINFORCING EMPLOYEE RESPONSIBILITY

Waste Management, like many companies, has been paternalistic in the traditional sense: we take seriously our responsibility to provide employees with a range of

benefits and a detailed explanation of how they can put those benefits to work effectively. Still, we had to go further, as the DOL's 404(c) regulations and recent interpretive guidelines made clear. What we needed was a way to reinforce employees' responsibility for maximizing their benefits, while giving them the information they needed to make their own decisions about personal financial matters.

More specifically, we were concerned about the concentration of 401(k) assets in the default fund, where contributions are automatically deposited if an employee does not choose a specific fund at enrollment. Until a few years ago, the default was a short-term income fund, not necessarily the best option for retirement savings. About 30% of our plan's assets remain in that fund; we want to encourage employees to be more active in choosing funds and managing their investments for long-term financial security.

Another concern was that employees who did not participate in the 401(k) were unclear about their company benefits and uncomfortable in general with money management concepts. They were skeptical about why the company wanted to take money from their paychecks now for a 401(k) plan that they couldn't touch until years later.

Waste Management wants as many employees as possible to participate in our 401(k) plan. Participation had been increasing over the past few years—up to about 70% from almost 60%—but senior management remains aware of the need to encourage even more employees to participate. In fact, the company has set participation goals for every division and progress in meeting these goals is one of the ways Waste Management measures each manager's performance and awards bonuses.

Driven by these concerns and goals, we decided that basic financial education made sense as a good way to help 401(k) non-participants understand their long-term financial responsibilities. It would also teach participating employees about the tools they could use to make more effective investment decisions. In fact, financial education would be part of an overall effort to make employees more aware of how they could use all available benefits to their best advantage, whether

they were saving for retirement, handling medical problems or addressing other benefits-related issues.

Although we have a lot of work ahead of us, we aren't starting from scratch. For some time, we have been distributing a steady stream of basic information about the 401(k) plan and its investment choices through a quarterly newsletter, booklets to new hires and a 401(k) video. These materials explain the differences among 401(k) investment funds and discuss the importance of saving for retirement. But we also realize that we have to go beyond our current communication efforts if we are going to persuade employees to assume a more active role in managing all their personal finances, not just retirement investments.

THE IDEAL PROGRAM

Even though we knew that we wanted to offer some kind of financial education program, we weren't sure what topics to cover or how to present the material. We began by establishing a task force of employees from the benefits area and the finance department to brainstorm about the ideal education program.

To guide the task force, we developed three specific goals for the education program: to improve the participation rate in the 401(k), help participants reallocate 401(k) plan assets to a more balanced mix and provide basic financial information in a format that would be accessible and understandable to all our employees.

Because we had no specific deadline for completing this project, the task force enjoyed the luxury of taking the time it needed to consider employees' needs thoroughly and do some "wish list" thinking about alternate ways to provide financial education. We wanted to get expert advice and invited a number of outside financial services suppliers to contribute their ideas about employee education and share with us the results of their independent research as it related to these issues.

TWO GROUPS, TWO SEMINARS

One issue that surfaced repeatedly during our planning was how to reach and motivate both participants and non-participants. Convinced that employees learn best when they can have personal interaction with a knowledgeable instructor, we considered how to offer seminars supplemented by information delivered through other media, including workbooks and videos. Because the attitudes and information needs of participants and non-participants were entirely different, we decided to divide the financial education program into two distinct parts.

We envisioned Financial Education I as a program for non-participants. It would be designed to encourage employees to save for the long-term and, equally important, motivate participation in the 401(k) as a tool to prepare for retirement. It would cover basic financial concepts, including types of investments, short and long-term investment goals, the magic of compounding, the impact of inflation, the importance of starting to save early for retirement and the ease of payroll savings. Although much of the message related to non-401(k) financial management, we also wanted to integrate key information about how the 401(k) plan works and the choice of fund options.

In contrast, Financial Education II would be geared to plan participants and provide more in-depth information about the basics of financial planning. The key messages would include the need to save more and the role of asset allocation. As program enhancements, we decided to include a self-test of individual risk tolerance, details about balancing risk and return, a discussion of retirement savings myths vs. realities and information about time horizons in the context of saving throughout life. Even though we expected this program to increase our employees' plan contributions and result in more diversified investments, we also wanted our employees to learn basic financial skills they can use in non-401(k) investments.

Next, we had to decide who would actually present the information. Given the close relationship we have with our 401(k) plan provider, we recognized that this company had the expertise to plan and conduct both seminars. We asked our plan provider to develop the content of the seminars, based on Waste Management's input about the specific needs of each group.

Pilot Seminars And Focus Groups

Working with our provider, we arranged the seminars as a pilot program in the Spring of 1996. Each seminar would last for two hours and include a workbook for attendees to use as they followed along with the instructor and at home for ongoing reinforcement of the concepts they learned in personal financial planning. To get maximum feedback, we held employee focus groups immediately following each seminar. This allowed us to hear attendees' comments, questions and suggestions on the content and format firsthand so we could tailor the education program to each group's specific needs.

After we sent out invitations—spouses were also invited to attend—we were amazed at the flood of employee responses. The first Financial Education II pilot filled up so quickly that, given the size of the room, we had to limit attendance. As part of the test, we offered one session of Financial Education I after hours and tried Financial Education II both during lunch (on-site) and in the evening (off-site).

Reluctance Vs. Enthusiasm

The pilot seminars revealed a stark contrast in reactions: we couldn't get the attendees at Financial Education I to stay; we couldn't get the attendees at Financial Education II to leave. In fact, both the lunchtime on-site seminar and the after-hours off-site Financial Education II seminars were well attended, indicating that timing and location had little or no significant impact on this group's attendance. We weren't surprised that the Financial Education I attendees, non-participants in the 401(k) plan, were a bit distrustful of the company's motives in inviting them to a meeting after the end of the work day. Interestingly, we became aware that none of these attendees came alone to this seminar: they either arrived with co-workers or brought their spouses. These attendees seemed reluctant to sit through the entire agenda; in fact, they appeared anxious to leave early. Clearly, we had to address the issue that an after-hours off-site group seminar did not seem to be a comfortable or convenient learning environment for non-participants, many of whom worked 55 to 60 hours per week and were not being paid for the time spent in the seminar.

The atmosphere at Financial Education II couldn't have been more different. Plan participants who attended these seminars were very enthusiastic and wanted to receive even more information. These employees were already receiving quarterly statements showing how their retirement savings were growing and they were eager to learn more about investment concepts.

Our perceptions of the employees' reactions were confirmed during the focus groups that followed each seminar. We asked attendees to describe the exercises they liked, the topics they wanted to spend more time on and the concepts they needed explained more clearly. Over and over again, employees said that they wanted somebody to tell them what they should do. Although we cannot offer advice, we recognize that providing more investment information will enable employees to make more informed decisions on their own.

We probed deeper during the focus groups, checking employees' knowledge of company benefits and the 401(k) plan in particular, which at Waste Management is coupled with a profit-sharing program. We discovered a number of non-participants who thought they were participating in the 401(k) when, in reality, their account statements reflected only profit-sharing payments. We were also surprised by non-participants' questions about what the company and the plan provider stood to gain from the 401(k) plan.

After analyzing the results of the pilot seminars and focus groups, weighing taskforce input and reviewing questions raised by employees who called our benefits office, we confirmed our belief that seminars alone would not meet all our employees' needs. Although seminars were well suited to the needs of plan participants, we had to go back to the drawing board to find a more comfortable way to interest non-participants in the basics of financial information.

PLANNING A COMPANY-WIDE PROGRAM

As we revisited the original proposal for financial education, we began to think in terms of delivering information through a range of media beyond seminars and reading materials. The content of Financial Education I was still valid, but we needed a more easily accessible medium to deliver the message, one that could get non-participants interested in financial education by enabling them to learn in the comfort of their own homes or work sites, and on their own schedules.

Our solution is to develop a 30-minute video for Financial Education I in place of the original seminar. We know that videos are user-friendly and employees can rewind and review sections as often as they want until they digest and understand the information. We plan to incorporate the basic concepts from Financial Education I into a video to be distributed along with a workbook for each employee. The Spanish-language versions of the video and the workbook will be produced after the English-language versions.

To accommodate the diversity of our employees and our number of locations, this program is being designed to allow each Waste Management division to decide how to use the video. One division might screen the video on company time at the worksite, while another might order copies to make available for employees to view at home. The workbook, which will cover types of investments, long and short-term financial goals and other fundamentals of financial planning, will help employees think about their risk tolerance and work out savings and asset allocation plans. It will include an evaluation form for employees to return that will help us gauge responses and continue to refine the program.

The PRISM 401(k) plan from Key is designed to help employees manage their 401(k) themselves. Our comprehensive array of educational materials and a 24-hour 800 number for balance and investment transfers put more control in their hands— and more time on yours. And PRISM offers a wide selection of fund options with a record of strong performance. To learn more about the benefits of PRISM, call 1-800-303-9826.

PRISM® 401(k) PLAN

More control for employees.
Less work for you.

Sounds like a plan.

Key. For a new America.℠

Despite the success of the seminar format for plan participants, we are considering testing a slightly different approach for Financial Education II. We may have our provider deliver the seminar in a live broadcast on WMX-TV, our in-house satellite broadcast television system—although divisions will still have the option to schedule an on-site seminar. The televised format will incorporate live interaction with employees at local sites, with the presenters addressing questions and comments from employees around the country.

Because our divisions can't completely close down operations to have all employees watch the seminar during a live broadcast, divisions will be able to videotape the broadcast for later or home-viewing. Employees can then call our provider's toll-free number if they have any questions. This is a flexible and inexpensive way to deliver financial education and, if we use this approach, we will follow up after the broadcast to learn how well this medium meets our employees' needs.

GETTING PERSONAL

Part of the challenge in making financial education available is to give employees the background they need to absorb information and ask relevant questions. We have recommended several systems enhancements that will allow every employee to receive a personalized booklet in advance of the local education effort, showing each employee's current profit-sharing account balance and, for participants, their 401(k) savings balance and investment mix. The booklets will provide general guidelines about saving for retirement and will indicate how the employee's current level of savings is likely to meet his or her retirement needs. Our overriding message is that employees need a long-term, well-planned savings program in order to retire comfortably.

Because of the strong request for personal assistance, we are building one-on-one interaction into our planned education program. This is where our provider comes into the picture again. Any employee who fills out the personal finance questionnaire after attending a financial education seminar or watching the broadcast will receive a free personalized investment report, as well as free telephone counseling from our provider about topics such as financial planning and asset allocation. Waste Management will pay for this service, which costs very little per employee, because we know that employees may have specific questions and need more personal counseling as they begin to implement what they learn during the seminar.

LOOKING AT THE BOTTOM LINE

Waste Management is planning a considerable investment in providing basic financial education to our diverse employee population. The first-year cost for production of the video, workbooks and the live seminar on WMX-TV will allow us to reach about 10,000 employees, one-third of the employees eligible for 401(k) participation, during that year.

We will not, however, rely solely on survey forms, focus groups and phone calls to gauge the success of our company-wide program once it is implemented. We have recommended that our systems group measure the increase over time of 401(k) participation and the changes in asset mix and contribution percentages.

We will then be able to compare allocation changes 24 to 36 months after starting the education process against the figures in place immediately before we kicked off the program. Using these quantitative measures, we will be able to gauge how well our employees are putting their new knowledge to work in managing their finances.

Our hope is that after the financial education program has been implemented, these measurements will show a steady increase in 401(k) participation and greater diversity in asset allocation among the funds. The real bottom line, however, is that our emphasis on basic financial education will help all employees—plan participants and non-participants alike—become more financially knowledgeable. They will be better prepared to make informed investment decisions to carry them securely through retirement and beyond.

 S M A R T   P I L L S

➤ Lay the groundwork for financial education seminars by providing personalized statements to each employee in advance.

➤ Set specific goals and decide how you will measure the results of various programs to determine what works and what needs improvement.

➤ Cover the basics in any financial education program.

➤ Tailor the education message and medium to each group's— participants and non-participants—unique situation.

➤ Consider the attitudes, reading level, language skills and comfort level of employees when determining the content and format of a financial education program.

➤ Provide an opportunity for one-on-one counseling to meet individual needs.

➤ Allow for flexibility in using different tools to deliver your educational message.

Experts Debate Employer Liability
And Total Financial Planning

P lan sponsors rarely talk about 401(k) education without voicing their concern over the potential for future liability. Understandably, those concerns multiply when they consider expanding their educational efforts to include a total financial education program that goes beyond the basics of explaining a 401(k) plan.

Many plan sponsors continue to struggle with a central issue: Where does education stop and advice begin? They ask how they can avoid crossing what most agree is still a blurred line and look for a government agency to give them some straight talk on employee education programs that teach financial planning in a non-401(k) context. The search for these answers raises other fundamental issues. Will this concern about liability extend indefinitely or will "advice" ultimately become acceptable? Most compellingly, plan sponsors ask themselves why they should provide financial education if they risk potential liability by doing so?

The Department of Labor (DOL) has long been aware that employers struggle to find the answers to these questions. In an effort to allay employers' concerns that by providing investment education to participants of self-directed individual account retirement plans they might actually be giving investment advice under ERISA's definition of a fiduciary, the DOL issued Interpretive Bulletin 96-1, Participant Investment Education, Final Rule in June 1996.

IB 96-1 sends a clear message that the DOL encourages employers to educate their employees, at least to the extent that those employees can then make informed investment and retirement-related decisions. The DOL also recognizes that to make informed investment and retirement-related decisions, employees must assess and understand their total financial picture. It follows, then, that the DOL would view total financial planning programs as appropriate tools to meet an important employee population need.

But the bottom line is that ERISA only regulates education programs covering 401(k) or other self-directed individual account retirement plans. ERISA does not regulate general financial education programs for employees. No government agency oversees or pays much attention to your classes on how to escape consumer debt, pay for your child's college education or care for your elderly parent—unless you cross the line and start offering investment advice. If you do, and you're talking about assets outside 401(k) or other self-directed individual account retirement plans, you may be moving into the supervisory orbit of the Securities and Exchange Commission (SEC), which regulates investment advisors.

If you offer your employees financial education to help them achieve lifelong financial security, it's virtually impossible to avoid the topic of retirement. How can you unbundle the various regulations, figure out where ERISA applies and know when you are in danger of crossing the line separating education and advice?

Investors Press developed a list of the questions plan sponsors ask most frequently on these issues and presented them to a panel of distinguished industry experts who discussed them in a Roundtable intended to give our readers some real answers. Bette Briggs, Chief of Fiduciary Interpretations with the Pension Welfare Benefits Administration at the Department of Labor,[1] joined R. Theodore Benna, hailed as the "father of the 401(k)" and founder and president of The 401(k) Association; Stephen Saxon, a partner with Groom & Nordberg, a Washington, D.C.-based employee benefits and tax firm; and Lou DeMattei, Benefits Tax Counsel and advisor on tax and ERISA issues at California-based Intel Corporation.

The wisdom shared by these employee benefits experts shows that the final word on these complicated issues has yet to be written. One thing is clear, however: each of our panelists acknowledges a pervasive need for a broader employee financial education. They agree that employers will determine what level of financial education is best for their companies and employees on a case by case basis—although Ted Benna believes that giving advice will eventually become an acceptable choice, leading many plan sponsors to cross the education line and offer employees the investment guidance it seems they truly want and need.

QUESTIONS & ANSWERS

Why should plan sponsors give employees a broad financial education? Wouldn't it be easier—with less risk of liability—to offer the minimum 401(k) information and let it go at that?

Stephen Saxon: Speaking purely from a liability standpoint, it would make the most sense to stick strictly to the disclosure requirements set forth in the regulations under 404(c).

Ted Benna: But the only way to guarantee absolutely no liability is to have no plan at all. 404(c) is not a utopia. Assuming that 404(c) frees you from liability exposure is far from the truth. More important, employees want and need more basic information and plan sponsors are going to be better off over the long-run by providing more, rather than less, educational support for their participants.

Stephen Saxon: I agree that many participants really do need basic information that explains things like what is a stock, what is a bond, what impact does infla-

---

[1] The views expressed by Ms. Briggs are her personal views and do not necessarily represent those of the Department of Labor.

tion have on my future plans. I think that participant education programs can be beneficial to participants and ought to be encouraged. IB 96-1 does exactly that.

Bette Briggs: The DOL recognizes that many employees are not planning adequately for retirement. Too often, employees have been given investment responsibility before they understand the basics—how to budget, save, determine their retirement needs, how to understand the benefits of tax-deferred saving and compound interest or the importance of making a thorough risk-reward analysis before choosing investment alternatives.

Section 404(c) relieves fiduciaries from responsibility for participant-directed investments if participants exercise independent control over the assets in their individual accounts. It requires, among other things, that in order for participants to exercise independent control, they must have sufficient information to make informed investment decisions. This includes certain descriptive information about the nature and operation of the plan and the various investment alternatives offered by the plan, but it doesn't include investment advice or education.

However, even though there is no requirement under 404(c) for employers to provide their employees with a financial or investment education, the DOL encourages employers to do so. The Interpretive Bulletin makes clear that providing a general investment education in the manner it describes will not affect the availability of relief under Section 404(c).

Lou DeMattei: I agree with Ted that the ERISA protection offered by Section 404(c) is limited. Employers who refrain from providing information authorized under IB 96-1 are probably doing their participants a disservice without significantly improving their protection against liability. In fact, to meet the "safe harbor" conditions of IB 96-1, plan sponsors are required specifically to instruct participants to consider all of their assets, including those held outside the plan, in determining the appropriate asset allocation for the 401(k) plan.

As an example, Intel offers guidance to 401(k) plan participants consistent with the "safe harbors" offered by the DOL that include some investment education. The decision to offer some investment education was made easier since Intel already had fiduciary liability for the prudent investment of its profit-sharing plan assets. In effect, Intel manages profit-sharing plan assets as an index fund (S&P) and its 401(k) plan offers an S&P 500 Fund investment option.[2] A plan sponsor

---

[2] Intel manages the profit-sharing plan investments with the objective of meeting or exceeding the S&P index rate of return. The objective can be accomplished either through investing directly in the S&P 500 basket of stocks, or if circumstances warrant, synthetically through the use of swaps and options contracts. At maturity, the profit-sharing plan nets the S&P 500 rate of return plus some additional kicker (e.g., 40 basis points).

The point is that the profit-sharing plan is invested, in effect, in the S&P 500 Fund and one of the 401(k) investment options available to participants is a provider's S&P Index Fund. Since Intel, as plan sponsor, has already decided that the S&P Index meets ERISA's prudence standard of being diversified sufficiently to minimize the risk of large losses, making a recommendation to invest 401(k) assets in the S&P 500, while not acceptable under either 404(c) or the Interpretative Bulletin, would not be such an increase to Intel's liability exposure as it would be for a plan that does not manage any retirement plan assets and has not taken a position with respect to the overall prudence of any investment.

Employee Benefit Research Institute
2121 K Street NW, Suite 600
Washington, DC 20037-1896

 ahead of change

Helping you stay

plan for the future

Helping you anticipate and

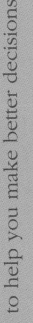

to help you make better decisions

for employee benefits research

EBRI
EMPLOYEE
BENEFIT
RESEARCH
INSTITUTE

Providing strategic information

The premier organization

For membership information call
Dallas L. Salisbury, President
(202) 775–6322
http://www.EBRI.com

"Hello, XYZ Company, this is your 35-year ex-employee, Joe Fox. I've got your
human resources manager here and, until I get the million-dollar nest egg I thought
I was going to get, he's going to be eating with me and my cat!"

who has not already assessed the general prudence of certain investments might
have had more reluctance to engage in employee education.

We also looked at, but rejected, a suggestion that the company specifically recommend investments in a 401(k) plan fund which replicates the profit-sharing
plan rate of return. Although the suggestion was rejected, it was based on the
premise that the fund meet general standards of prudence to which the company
is already being held.

Do 404(c) and Interpretive Bulletin 96-1 specifically cover financial education that goes beyond the 401(k)?

Stephen Saxon: If an education program includes a financial planning component
that looks at all an employee's assets, including 401(k) or other retirement savings
vehicles, such as IRAs, Federal law in the form of ERISA regulations will apply to
the retirement assets. However, ERISA will not apply for the non-retirement assets.

Do you mean that the safe harbors that apply to financial and investment education under ERISA don't protect employers once they start talking about non-401(k) savings?

Stephen Saxon: Well, let's be clear here about our terms. ERISA applies to
employers who have federally regulated retirement plans and offer their employees
education to help them invest their plan assets wisely. ERISA does not concern
itself with regulating non-retirement savings and as such, there is no ERISA liability associated with communications unrelated to ERISA covered plans.

By its terms, IB 96-1 only covers the provision of information in participant-
directed individual account retirement plans. As such, it would not cover circumstances where participants cannot exercise investment control over the plan's
investment. IB 96-1 also would not cover the information provided with respect

to traditional DB plans. However, the analysis of IB 96-1 makes clear that the provision of plan information and general financial information should not raise ERISA fiduciary issues in any circumstance. While IB 96-1 does not extend to other retirement plans or other assets, it's important to note that the Bulletin expressly requires that participants be informed that they should consider all their other assets in retirement planning. Certainly, nothing in IB 96-1 should preclude an employer from providing broader financial counseling beyond a typical 401(k) plan. But, if you are offering people information or advice on how to invest all their savings, including those in federally regulated retirement savings vehicles, then you should take SEC regulations into account because, as an employer, you probably do not want to be considered an investment advisor.

The definition of investment advisor under ERISA is different than its definition under the securities laws. For example, financial institutions (service providers) offering participant education as a part of a 401(k) product may be subject to regulation as investment advisors under the securities laws, but would not be investment advisors (fiduciaries) under ERISA to the extent that they fit within the safe harbors of the Interpretive Bulletin.

How does ERISA describe an investment advisor for 401(k) purposes?

Bette Briggs: Under the regulations, a person who makes recommendations to a participant as to the advisability of investing in, purchasing or selling securities or other property will be considered to be rendering investment advice if such advice is provided on a regular basis, pursuant to a mutual understanding that the advice will serve as a primary basis for the participant's plan investment decisions and will be based on the particular needs of the participant.

Stephen Saxon: An important point to keep in mind here is that in order for investment-related information to constitute investment advice all those criteria must be satisfied.

Does ERISA say what isn't considered to be investment advice?

Bette Briggs: The Interpretive Bulletin identifies four broad categories of information, or safe harbors, that do not constitute "investment advice" under ERISA's "fiduciary" definition—provided the conditions of the safe harbors are met. The first two safe harbors cover general plan and financial or investment information. This includes, for example, information about the investment philosophies of any investment funds offered by the plan, or how the different investment options are categorized by asset class based on risk and return characteristics. The last two safe harbors cover asset allocation information provided through the use of hypothetical models or interactive materials, such as questionnaires and worksheets or computer programs.

Stephen Saxon: The Bulletin also specifies that these four safe harbors are non-exclusive. In other words, information not specifically mentioned would not necessarily constitute investment advice under ERISA. Each case must be analyzed individually based on its own facts and circumstances.

To
know us
is to
know

The key is to give the participant sufficient information so that he or she can make informed investment decisions. Specifically, IB 96-1 says that a plan sponsor is not rendering investment advice by giving participants information and materials about general financial and investment concepts such as risk and return, diversification, dollar cost averaging, compound return and tax-deferred investments. Nor are you rendering advice by telling your employees about the historic differences in rates of return between different asset classes based on standard market indices, explaining the effects of inflation or giving them the information or tools they need to estimate future retirement income needs, determine investment time horizons or assess risk tolerance. In other words, you're okay if you give the basic tools they need to make a financial plan.

Lou DeMattei: IB 96-1 is very permissive in that it contemplates that plan sponsors could provide educational materials not specifically addressed in the Bulletin without necessarily rendering investment advice. The key point plan sponsors should remember is that if 404(c) protection is desired, they should not make specific recommendations to participants.

 How does the SEC describe an investment advisor?

Stephen Saxon: The term "investment advisor" is generally defined under the Investment Advisors Act of 1940 to mean any person who, for compensation, engages in the business of advising others, either directly or through writings and publications, as to the value of securities or as to the advisability of investment in securities. The definition of investment advisor under the securities laws is generally regarded as broader than the ERISA definition.

Does the employer have liability if it employs outside advisors to give classes? Even if it indemnifies itself to employees when it hires an outside expert as a surrogate educator?

Ted Benna: Employers can make sure they have an indemnification agreement with any vendor providing support. Communicate clearly to your employees that the vendor is offering suggestions to help them with future planning, but whether or not to act on the advice is up to the employee. You might say something like, "We are providing this financial planning program because we want to help our employees. We would never run our pension plan without professional support and we feel that you shouldn't be flying blind without professional support when it comes to your financial planning. How you use this help is, of course, totally up to you."

Stephen Saxon: You can protect yourself by issuing a disclaimer such as Ted has suggested. You can say, "We are making this service available but we take no responsibility for the advice." Basically, you are telling employees "Caveat Emptor".

However, if the employer explicitly assumes a duty to monitor the provider on an ongoing basis and represents to employees that it is doing so and does not follow through, there is potential liability exposure. For example, there may be future problems if the provider is incompetent or has a conflict of interest.

What if a financial planner gives bad advice?

Stephen Saxon: If it involves retirement funds, assuming the advice is covered by one of the safe harbors in IB 96-1, this should not be an ERISA issue. However, the Bulletin makes clear that you have a duty, as an employer, to monitor your service providers. In addition, other laws, such as the securities laws, may come into play.

 What if an employee attends a class, for example, on how to pay for a child's college education, then comes back and sues the company because he or she ends up not being able to afford to send the child to college after all?

Bette Briggs: If employers are not in the business of giving financial advice, they would not be considered to be investment advisors under the Investment Advisors Act of 1940 merely because they provide the type of investment education described in IB 96-1. The DOL specifically consulted the SEC about this.

 Under IB 96-1, does it make any difference how you provide the education: videos versus a computer software program versus a one-on-one planning session, for example?

Stephen Saxon: Technically, IB 96-1 says it doesn't matter. You can use written materials, videos, even interactive computer programs. You can present the material as often as you like. You can present it in group meetings or during one-on-one counseling sessions. However, the potential for a counselor to cross the line and give advice is greater and more difficult to monitor in person-to-person situations.

Bette Briggs: The DOL recognizes that investment education is more effective when participants have the opportunity to examine their own situations. As Steve mentioned, in one-on-one counseling sessions there may be more of a temptation to cross the line and give advice so, as a practical matter, it may be safer for the employer to use other methods. Keep in mind that you don't necessarily need one-on-one counseling to provide personalized educational materials. The Bulletin's safe harbors for asset allocation models and interactive investment materials recognize the value of educational materials that enable individuals to consider their own outcomes under different scenarios.

Lou DeMattei: There is wide latitude here in how you provide the education. The material that Intel provides to its 401(k) participants consists of three basic elements. We provide brochures which describe the general benefits of saving in tax-deferred retirement plans, explain different concepts of risk and show basic asset classes. We also provide a brochure that describes the investment options available to 401(k) participants and ranks their levels of risk.

Participants also receive an "Investor Profile Questionnaire", which they can complete to help them understand what level of risk they are comfortable with and, ultimately, what asset allocation is most appropriate for them. The entire package is designed to give participants the tools they need to make intelligent decisions that are appropriate for them without our making specific recommendations.

In addition to material related to the 401(k) plan, Intel regularly presents general retirement planning seminars in conjunction with the AARP. These seminars, open to all employees, cover a wide range of topics beside investment planning. The investment component, although general, takes an approach somewhat similar to the one provided to 401(k) participants. General asset categories are explained and attendees are given the opportunity to assess the appropriate level of risk for themselves. All of these approaches are acceptable under IB 96-1.

 But if you give participants asset allocation models based on their particular circumstances, doesn't that cross over the line from education to investment advice?

Stephen Saxon: If the criteria in the safe harbors are satisfied, then according to IB 96-1, asset allocation models based on individual financial information will not constitute "investment advice" for ERISA purposes. For example, the Bulletin's safe harbor for interactive materials clearly contemplates that participants will be able to specify variables in a computer program that reflect their actual circumstances. The key is to give participants the tools they need to analyze a broad spectrum of information so that they can make informed investment decisions.

Lou DeMattei: That's right. This is educational material. The employee still needs to make the final decision to take action one way or another.

What are the criteria for asset allocation models?

Stephen Saxon: An asset allocation model must be based on generally accepted investment theories that take into account historic returns of different asset classes. The model has to disclose the assumptions on which it is based, such as retirement age, income, inflation and rates of return. If the model identifies any specific investment alternatives in the plan, it has to also state that other investment alternatives might be available in the plan and tell people where to get more information about them.

Also, as Lou has mentioned, the model must be accompanied by a statement telling participants that, when making allocation decisions, they should consider their other assets, income and investments, such as home equity and savings accounts, in addition to their assets in the plan.

Bette Briggs: I couldn't have put it better myself. In fact, the safe harbor for interactive investment materials expressly contemplates that participants will use computerized or other programs to generate multiple asset allocation models based on their own particular circumstances. The theory is that as long as the assumptions underlying the models are revealed and the other criteria of the safe harbor are met, participants will be able to assess independently the relevance of the models to their own circumstances.

Stephen Saxon: Safe Harbor Four (Interactive Computer Programs) envisions the use of personal financial data. Under this safe harbor, a program can even identify the specific funds available in various asset categories.

LET METLIFE GUIDE YOUR 401(k) INVESTMENT CHOICES.

MetLife's full service 401(k) program addresses both the demand for investment choice and the need for improved participant education.

Our comprehensive investment menu offers you extensive flexibility with the information and know-how to use it. Whether you choose some of today's best known mutual funds from our MetSelect Alliance℠ or prefer the institutional approach of our unique MetLife/UAM program,* we provide the guidance you need to offer the most appropriate funding choices for your participants.

Our informed choice approach will change the way your participants think about 401(k) investing. Let MetLife help you create the optimum investment program for your 401(k) plan. Call us at 1-800-722-6091.

EDUCATE-COMMUNICATE
Defined Contribution Group
✳ MetLife®

*Group annuity contracts issued by Metropolitan Life Insurance Co., NY, NY

Mutual funds offered through MetSelect Alliance by MetLife Securities, Inc., One Madison Ave., NY, NY 10010. MetLife receives a fee from the fund families for providing certain administrative and record-keeping services for the funds.

SCHULZ

Lou DeMattei: IB 96-1 notes that interactive materials enable employees to base several possible asset allocation models on individual circumstances, but that these are not sufficiently different from hypothetical models to pose a problem. They will not constitute advice.

Ted Benna: Everyone is so concerned about stepping over the line to give investment advice, but I think the line is going to get blown away. The fact is, employees want advice. They want someone to tell them what funds to invest in and how much to put in each fund; they don't just want asset allocation models.

Right now, financial planning—in the sense that you provide participants with a specific investment strategy—is a controversial area in the 401(k) world. I think a fair amount of emotion is going to center around it. But, five years from now, we'll ask ourselves why this was such an emotional issue, because in reality this is what participants want and need. It reminds me of the controversy that surrounded daily valuation. Five years ago, that was all you heard. Plan sponsors were very concerned that if participants had access to daily valuation, they would start market-timing or trade irresponsibly. In the vast majority of cases, that hasn't happened. It's a non-issue today and giving employees investment advice will be a non-issue, as well.

 What do you think of Ted's prediction about investment advice?

Lou DeMattei: I think that plan sponsors, particularly those with investment funds offering their own stock, will be more reluctant to accept the role of investment advisor than they have been to accept the notion of daily valuations. The opposition to daily valuations may have been based on a misperception about how employees would use—or abuse—them, and ultimately, acceptance of them was driven by market factors. Plan sponsors will continue to have concerns about their exposure to employee and shareholder lawsuits if they directly engage in advice to employees. I think these legal concerns will persist despite a permissive atmosphere concerning employee education.

I do think that some other factors support Ted's view, however. Plan sponsors will see increasing employee interest in the availability of brokerage accounts within the 401(k) context. If it is clear that the investment advice is provided by an independent third party, as would be possible with a brokerage account, the plan sponsor's concerns about being cast in the role of investment advisor will be substantially reduced, if not eliminated.

Stephen Saxon: To the extent an employer or a financial institution hired by an employer offers investment advice and, as such, is an ERISA fiduciary, issues arise from a liability standpoint and from an ERISA prohibited transaction standpoint. First, as a fiduciary, the investment advisor could be held personally liable under ERISA to the extent that the advice provided was, for example, imprudent. Secondly, because the advice given may affect the amount of compensation paid from mutual funds in the form of 12b-1 or administrative service fees, such advice could raise conflicts of interest or potential self-dealing under ERISA's fiduciary responsibility provisions.

ONLY METLIFE GUARANTEES TO INCREASE YOUR 401(k) PLAN PARTICIPATION.

With MetLife's MetAssure,℠ if your plan participation is not reaching the levels we agree upon up front, then we automatically work with you until we meet those levels, at no additional charge.

It's the MetLife Participation Guarantee, and it's just one of the many innovative features you'll find in our acclaimed education and communication process.

For more information on the MetAssure Participation Guarantee or to learn more about our extraordinary education emphasis, call us at 1-800-722-6091 or e-mail: 401(k) info @ metlife.com.

EDUCATE - COMMUNICATE
Defined Contribution Group

✳ MetLife®

SCHULZ
PEANUTS © United Feature Syndicate, Inc.

For example, if under the plan document the employer is responsible for paying the costs of operating a plan, and the employer, as a fiduciary, offers investment advice that influences participants to select a mutual fund investment option that pays a higher administrative service fee, the advice could be deemed to be an act of self-dealing under ERISA. So, employers ought to review carefully their plan document before they engage in providing investment advice.

Similar conflicts can arise in the context of investment advice provided by financial institutions that are hired by employers. If the advice given by the institution could affect the institution's compensation, issues will arise under ERISA's fiduciary responsibility provisions. In such cases, the institution may have to rely on an exemption granted by the DOL.

 Any closing comments or observations?

Lou DeMattei: I think the DOL's Interpretive Bulletin is a strong indication that it favors employee financial education provided by plan sponsors. Employer's circumstances vary, but I believe that all employers should at least review their employee communications related to 401(k) investments and see whether some enhancement is appropriate. Most employers will probably find that following the safe harbors in the guidelines is possible.

Stephen Saxon: What this all boils down to is an employer's prudent management of risk—the chief risk being that the employer could be held responsible and liable for investment decisions made by employees. ERISA's regulations, including IB 96-1, provide some guidance on how to manage these risks. While ERISA does not apply to all of an employee's assets, it may, nevertheless, make sense for employers to adopt some of ERISA's basic principles for all assets to which an education program applies. The more basic of these principles is that employers will be best protected, and employees will be served, if employees make truly informed judgments about their investments. In the long run, therefore, a proactive employer—one who provides meaningful education and assistance—will have less concern about the ability of employees to cope successfully with the rigors and financial burdens of retirement.

Bette Briggs: There is a compelling need for participant education. Employees are being asked to assume greater responsibility for ensuring the adequacy of their retirement income, but the evidence shows that many are not planning and saving sufficiently. All too often, employees don't participate fully in their employer's retirement plans. When they do participate, they tend to be risk averse and overly conservative in their investment choices. Billions of dollars of potential retirement savings are lost when lump sum distributions are spent, rather than rolled over into an IRA or another retirement plan.

The key to financial security in retirement is education. Employees need to know their retirement needs; to appreciate compound interest and how retirement plans maximize savings by deferring taxes; to understand basic investment principles and realize that the vast majority of investment returns—90% by some estimates—is attributable to diversification, the selection of broad asset categories, rather than the selection of individual investments; to appreciate the importance of not dipping into retirement savings and of rolling over the plan assets into an IRA or their new employer's retirement account if they change jobs.

Under the safe harbors described in Interpretive Bulletin 96-1, employers can provide participant investment education without fear of assuming fiduciary liability for their employees' investment decisions. The DOL encourages employers to take full advantage of the safe harbors in IB 96-1: inform employees about the investments offered under their retirement plans; explain basic retirement planning and investment principles; illustrate outcomes using hypothetical asset allocation models; and offer computerized programs or other interactive materials that give employees the opportunity to develop and test their own asset allocation models to determine their individual retirement needs.

Top Tips On Saving, Investing And Spending From Leading Financial Planners Nationwide

Financial security—everybody wants it, but most of us are confused about how to find it. The answer isn't making a killing on Wall Street or finding the once in a lifetime investment that turns to gold. The Midas touch is in setting realistic goals for today and tomorrow, saving enough money to get you through a crisis and learning to live within your means.

Since none of us is born with the financial management skills we need, Investors Press asked a group of the nation's top financial planners to help our readers get smarter about how to achieve lifetime financial security.[1] Drawing on what their vast experience has taught them, they offer the top tips we all need to know about money and finances. Setting the stage for the best suggestions you can pass along to your employees is an important and reassuring insight from Kathy Kristof, syndicated personal finance columnist at *The Los Angeles Times* known as "the new Sylvia Porter". She reminds us all that achieving financial security is indeed a lifetime process—it does not and cannot happen overnight.

1. Relax. Financial peace of mind can be reached at almost any income level. Decide what's important to you and set some goals. Remember that without concrete numbers, goal setting is nothing more than dreaming. Having a real idea of where you want to go will help you get there. You don't have to be a math whiz and you don't need an MBA to do this—just take a deep breath and take the first step.

---

[1] In compiling this list of top financial tips, Investors Press interviewed financial planners chosen by *Worth* magazine for its October 1996 list of the nation's top 200 financial planners. Among those who provided tips are Steven Ames, Annapolis, Maryland; Sidney Blum, Mayer, Kolof & Lev, Deerfield, Illinois; Mary Katherine Dean, Dean Consulting & Associates, San Diego, California; David Kahn, Goldstein Golub Kessler & Company, P.C., New York, New York; Dorothy Lebeau, Lebeau Financial Advisory, Jenkinstown, Pennsylvania; Judith Martindale, San Luis Obispo, California; Vincent Schiavi, Wilmington, Delaware and Virginia Stanley, Albuquerque, New Mexico.

SAVE AS MUCH AS YOU CAN—AS EARLY AS YOU CAN!

2 Remember that saving early in life is the best thing you can do. You can take advantage of the magic of compounding over a long period of time and end up with a lot of money. You are never too old to start. No matter when you start to save, you'll have more financial security than if you don't save at all.

3 Concentrate on a simple formula: *spend less than you make and save as much as you can as early as you can.* Pay yourself first. Money experts can't stress this enough. Find a way to put money away for your short and long-term goals before you spend it. You won't miss the money you save if you don't see it and you'll be thrilled to see how quickly the money you save grows into a healthy nest egg. Many financial planners recommend saving 10% of your income each month. Think you can't do it? Then save 5%. Save 1% if that is all you can really afford, but don't wait until you earn more to start saving. The point is: start now and make saving automatic.

> **Examples of automatic savings programs include:**
> - depositing payroll deductions directly to your savings account or a company-sponsored retirement plan
> - authorizing a mutual fund company to automatically debit your savings/checking account each month

4 Look for clues that you are living beyond your means. You can't save 10% of your earnings. You can't pay off your credit card balances each month. You have to scramble to pay taxes, auto registration and insurance. You lose sleep worrying about bills.

If any one or several of these clues apply to you, it's time to remind yourself that your financial independence will not take care of itself. You can't leave it to chance. Take charge of your financial future by learning about basic financial management concepts and personalizing them to your lifestyle.

5 Consider your budget carefully long before you retire. Don't underestimate expenses. Those rosy old days when companies financed our retirement are over. Now it's up to each one of us to protect our own financial future. Go through your records for the last year or so and list all your expenses, including those related to investment accounts and gifts. Consider any special expenses you may have after retirement, including medical, travel and long-term care insurance. Calculate inflation and investment returns that will be reinvested. Make sure your current savings give you a comfortable margin for emergencies. Consider saving more and/or working longer, if possible.

BE SMART: THINK AHEAD!

6 Keep track of your long-term finances by calculating and monitoring your "net worth": your assets (the equity in your house, your savings and investments) minus your liabilities (your debts). Measure your investment performance to see if you are making progress in reaching your goals. **Do this at least once a year.**

If your assets aren't increasing and/or your liabilities aren't decreasing, you need to reevaluate and restructure your financial program.

7 Consider prepaying high-interest installment debt, including credit cards and bank loans. Saving interest is a lot like earning interest. You can build your net worth, and your nest egg, by increasing your assets (savings) and reducing your liabilities—in particular, your high-interest debt. By continuing to borrow for non-essential expenditures, you run the risk of never retiring the principal balance on your loans and never generating the disposable income necessary to maintain a savings program.

8 Focus on career security, not job security. Develop skills that will make you marketable for other, or higher, paying jobs. Don't get stuck working in a job that makes it hard for you to transfer to another employer.

9 Before you concern yourself with investment issues, build a sufficient cash reserve and give yourself the risk protection you'll need (life, disability and health insurance) for unexpected expenses. Many financial planners suggest that you keep liquid assets equal to three to six months of your living costs in a savings account or money market fund for such emergencies.

TAKE ADVANTAGE OF YOUR 401(k)!

10 Always participate in employer savings programs **at least** to the fullest extent the employer will match. This is the greatest low-risk investment around.

11 Stay away from investments you don't understand. If it seems too good to be true, it usually is. If it's too complicated to understand, you shouldn't be risking your money. Non-traditional investments such as collectibles, real estate limited partnerships, commodities, precious metals and investment-oriented life insurance products rarely achieve the returns they promise and often accomplish little more than generating commission income for those selling these products.

12 Diversify! Put your long-term investments into more than one type of investment vehicle. Research indicates that diversification is the most important decision driving overall investment returns. Having CDs in several banks does not mean you are diversified. You must invest in different asset classes, such as cash, stocks and bonds.

13 Don't try to "time" the financial markets. You'll almost always be wrong. What goes up must come down, and what goes down usually goes back up. But nobody knows when those market changes will happen. Invest regularly in up markets and down markets, a risk management strategy the pros call dollar cost averaging.

If you are a long-term investor, you'll see many natural and unavoidable market ups and downs. This doesn't mean you should ignore your investments once you make them. Look at comparable investments. If, for example, a particular mutual fund underperforms the major market averages for more than a year, consider investing that money in another fund.

14 When you consider various investment options, don't look only at yields. Consider total returns on investments. This includes the annual payments received, plus any increase in the value of the investment. Remember that appreciation—the amount the value of the investment goes up—is taxed only when the investments are sold.

15 When you invest in mutual funds, don't look only at the return a fund is getting today; check the one, three and five-year performance of each fund.

16 Be sure to consider the effect of income tax on all your investments, including those in your retirement plan. Taxes will reduce the actual amount you keep. Generally, retirement funds are taxable at ordinary rates on 100% of the withdrawal. Other investments will be taxed only on the capital gains (what you get when you sell, less what you originally paid and any commissions or other sales-related expenses).

17 Check for hidden fees: you have a right to know how much it will cost you to buy and/or sell an investment. If you buy stocks, bonds or mutual funds through a broker, be sure you understand how much it will really cost you to make the purchase. Will you pay a commission up front? When you sell? When you buy and sell?

THINK BEFORE YOU ACT!

18 Don't pay more taxes than you have to. It's crucial to manage your tax obligations and pay the least amount permitted by law. Start your tax planning in January every year: know what is tax deductible and keep good records. Take advantage of any tax-saving programs offered through your employer, such as tax-advantaged retirement plans (401(k) plans and special savings plans that allow you to save pre-tax money each month for specific expenses, such as child care or health-related costs).

If you aren't eligible for a tax-advantaged savings plan through your employer, consider saving with an IRA.

19 If you are thinking about buying a "house" instead of a starter home, save your money and buy a house your family can be comfortable in for at least ten years. In most of the country, housing prices are growing at a much slower rate than in the recent past. That means it will take many years for a starter home to appreciate enough in value so that you can afford to sell it and buy a bigger house.

Convincing employees to save for retirement can be an uphill battle. Don't fight it alone.

The American Savings Education Council can help. We're a coalition of more than 200 private and public sector institutions—including IBM, American Express, Bankers Trust, Fidelity, EBRI, ICI, ACLI, ReliaStar, VALIC, U.S. Department of Labor and U.S. Department of the Treasury—dedicated to raising public awareness about the importance of planning for long-term, personal financial independence.

As an institutional partner of ASEC, you would have an ally in your efforts to promote saving and retirement planning to your employees. Our brochures—"The Power to Choose," "Top 10 Ways to Beat the Clock and Prepare for Retirement," and "How Do I Get to There From Here?"—can help you educate your employees about saving and planning. We also offer "Ballpark," an easy-to-use worksheet that your employees can use to get a rough idea of how much they'll need to save for retirement.

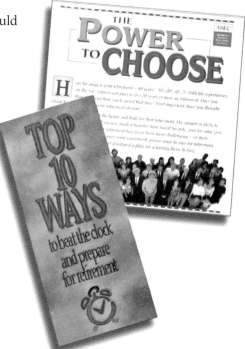

The brochures, worksheet and other educational tools are available to your institution when you join ASEC. Through your ASEC affiliation, you would show your employees that you take their saving and planning needs seriously.

ASEC would be stronger with your institution as a partner. As an ASEC partner, you would play a key role in helping us expand our national public awareness campaign. We would actively enlist your support, drawing on your expertise for ideas and suggestions.

Become an ASEC Partner.

For information about joining the American Savings Education Council, call ASEC President Don Blandin at (202) 775-9130 or ASEC Chairman Dallas Salisbury at (202) 659-0670. And be sure to visit our Web site. The battle for your employees' financial future is on. And we're up for the fight.

American Savings Education Council
Suite 600 · 2121 K Street NW · Washington, DC 20037-1896
Tel: (202) 775-9130 or (202) 659-0670 · Fax: (202) 775-6312
Web Site: www.asec.org

ASEC is part of the EBRI Education and Research Fund.

ASEC
AMERICAN
SAVINGS
EDUCATION
COUNCIL

20 Make additional principal payments whenever you can afford it if you expect to stay in your home for a long time. Sending an extra $25 with your mortgage payment each month results in a saving of tens of thousands of dollars in interest over the life of your mortgage. This is especially true in the early years of your mortgage.

21 Remember that life insurance protects families when the wage-earner(s) dies. Buying lots of term insurance when you are young and have small children will help generate adequate income for those you leave behind until they can support themselves.

Don't waste premium dollars on insuring the lives of your children. That money is better spent on increasing the insurance on the family's breadwinners.

22 Make a will and keep it up to date. If you die without a will, the state in which you live will determine how your property will be divided. Your surviving spouse may not inherit everything you had intended and property will not go to non-relatives and/or to specific charities as you may have wished. Beyond that, a will allows you to select a legal guardian for your children, appoint the executor or trustee of your choice and provide for special wishes and bequests to close friends or children from a previous marriage.

23 Make financial peace of mind a family affair. Teach your children about financial responsibility and the importance of saving when they are young and can practice with something as simple as their allowance. Building the habit of saving into appropriate behavior is a lesson your children will thank you for long into their lives.

In this age of the growing "sandwich generation", when baby boomers are often responsible for their children *and* their parents, discussing money matters with parents can also be a very good idea. Families who coordinate estate planning can pass on financial benefits for generations to come.

THE RESOURCE GUIDE IS A SERIES OF SPECIAL SECTIONS INTENDED TO ENHANCE THE EDUCATIONAL VALUE OF THIS BOOK AND EXTEND ITS USEFULNESS AS A REFERENCE TOOL AND RESOURCE.

➤ UNDERWRITER PROFILES

➤ ANNOTATED BIBLIOGRAPHY:
  FINANCIAL PLANNING
  RESOURCES FOR
  ALL EMPLOYEES

UNDERWRITER PROFILES

Allmerica Financial Institutional Services

A division of First Allmerica Financial Life Insurance Company
440 Lincoln Street, Worcester, MA 01653
1-800-853-AFIS

Key Contacts:
Charles Bevis, *Managing Director*

Organization: A subsidiary of the Allmerica Financial Corporation (a Fortune 500 company), AFIS is part of a family of companies who have a 150-year history of providing insurance protection and financial security to its clients. With over 50 years in the retirement industry, more than 850 clients, and $3.6 billion in institutional assets under management, AFIS' experience and resources provide a plan that maximizes plan participation and employee contributions while minimizing plan sponsor involvement.

AFIS offers a wide range of retirement and benefit products and asset management services, including:
- annuities and insurance
- retirement and employee benefit plans
- strategic and tactical distribution support
- asset management and trust services

Retirement Programs: AFIS offers a full range of retirement programs, including Allmerica Choice, a complete 401(k) plan. Choice reduces the plan sponsor's administrative and fiduciary burdens by emphasizing employee education; it offers a variety of investment options and provides high-level service for employers and employees.

Our employee education program includes an interactive multimedia enrollment presentation, workbooks and asset allocation worksheets and complete investment option information.

The Choice investment options are managed by some of the country's leading institutional and retail money managers, including Nicholas-Applegate Capital Management, Putnam Investments and Fidelity Investments. An independent evaluation committee monitors the performance and practices of the money managers to ensure consistent results through market cycles.

AFIS is committed to its clients: we design the right solutions through a consultative approach, provide superior customer service and offer a complete package of bundled services tailored to each client's needs.

American Century$_{SM}$ Investments

P.O. Box 419385, Kansas City, MO 64141

Key Contact:
American Century Investment Services, Inc.
800-988-9084

The Company: Combining the investment strengths of Twentieth Century Mutual Funds and The Benham Group, American Century Investments has emerged as a multidiscipline investment organization offering over 65 no-load mutual funds.

American Century offers full-service bundled recordkeeping, including investment management, administrative services and employee communications. We pride ourselves on our ability to provide our clients with a customized level of high-touch service. We are so committed to delivering the highest level of service and attention that our recordkeeping services are backed by an unconditional guarantee.

Investments: American Century offers a flexible menu of investment choices to meet the diverse needs of plan participants. These include:
- a broad range of no-load mutual funds
- asset allocation funds
- self-directed brokerage accounts that allow access to over 1,600 mutual funds, as well as individual securities.

Recordkeeping: American Century takes a consultative approach to recordkeeping services. We don't offer "canned" solutions. Instead, we analyze each client's needs and develop creative, customized solutions. Each of our clients works with a dedicated account representative who can respond to all their ongoing administrative needs, from loans to discrimination tests. We are so committed to service excellence, we make our entire client list available for reference checks.

Employee Education: Our new approach to developing educational materials for plan participants utilizes participant research, incorporates communications personalized to individual participants and listens to our clients: we create communication plans that get results.

American Express Financial Advisors Inc.

P. O. Box 489, Minneapolis, MN 55440-0489

Key Contacts

American Express
Institutional Services 1-800-437-0600
(A division of American Express Financial Advisors Inc.)
Ward Armstrong, *President* 612-671-1915
John C. Rowe,
National Sales Manager 612-671-7108

Year Founded 1894

Assets Under Management

	Clients	Assets
Total American Express Financial Advisors Inc.	1.9 M	$150.6 B
American Express Institutional Services	340 **	$13 B *
Custodial Assets		$84.5 B *

* As of 12/31/96; asset figures for American Express
Trust Company
** Corporate/institutional clients

Special Areas of Expertise: American Express
Institutional Services, a division of American
Express Financial Advisors Inc., along with
American Express Trust Company, offers the complete defined contribution/401(k) plan outsourcing
solution—from investments, trust and recordkeeping to employee education. American Express
Financial Advisors offers a range of mutual fund
products to both institutional and retail clients, all
developed and managed to represent the various
risk/return steps on the investment spectrum.
American Express Trust Company provides collective
funds specifically designed for qualified plans and
managed in compliance with ERISA. American
Express Trust Company also provides separate stable
capital account management services. Access to
outside money management is available to qualified
plan investors through out SmartPartners℠ alliance.

Investment Approach: We believe our approach is
well suited to the needs of retirement plan sponsors
and participants. By consistently applying the disciplined, hands-on management skills acquired
through more than 50 years in fund management,
American Express Financial Advisors seeks to manage investments without exposing plan participants
to more near-term volatility than is necessary to seek
to achieve the investment objective.

Founders Asset Management, Inc.

2930 East Third Avenue, Denver, CO 80206
Phone: 1-800-934-GOLD • Fax: 303-394-4021
Founders Investor*site* at www.founders.com

Key Contact Information:

Greg Contillo,
Senior Vice President 1-800-806-2986

Year founded: 1938

Total Assets Under Management From All Sources:

$5.3 billion (*as of February 1, 1997*)

Special Areas of Expertise: The Founders Funds
family of 11 no-load growth-oriented mutual funds
includes aggressive-growth, growth, international,
growth-and-income, and fixed-income offerings.

The Founders Family of Funds:

(listed in order from higher-risk/higher-return
potential to lower-risk/lower-return potential):

Fund	Category
Founders Discovery Fund	Micro-/Small-Cap
Founders Passport Fund	International Small-Cap
Founders Frontier Fund	Small-Cap
Founders Special Fund	Capital Appreciation
Founders International Equity Fund	Core International
Founders Worldwide Growth Fund	Global Equity
Founders Growth Fund	Mid-/Large-Cap
Founders Blue Chip Fund	Growth and Income
Founders Balanced Fund	Balanced
Founders Government Securities Fund	Government Securities
Founders Money Market Fund	Money Market

Fund news and portfolio manager commentary are
available on Founders *Insight*, 1-800-525-2440,
option 5, 24 hours a day.

Investment Approach: Founders Funds' *growth-style*
investment approach means we build equity portfolios
one stock at a time, searching for companies whose
fundamental strengths give them the potential to
provide superior earnings growth over time. Founders
finds these companies through intensive bottom-up
research: our portfolio managers meet with company
management, tour manufacturing facilities and visit
the company's suppliers and competitors to understand
every aspect of its business and industry. Furthermore,
we provide top-quality service and support that is
tailored to the specific needs of our clients.

John Hancock Funds

A Global Investment Management Firm
101 Huntington Avenue, Boston, MA 02199
1-800-294-7734 • Fax: 617-375-4710

Key Contacts:
James V. Bowhers,
 Executive Vice President 617-375-4880
Edward J. Lavelle,
 Senior Vice President, Retirement
 Sales and Client Service 617-375-4706

Year Founded: 1968

Total Assets Under Management: . . . $23 billion
As of 12/31/96

Organization: John Hancock Funds is a subsidiary of John Hancock Financial Services, one of the nation's leading financial services providers. With over $112 billion in assets under management, John Hancock has been providing financial security for customers since 1862. In today's complex financial environment, John Hancock is able to demonstrate exceptional financial strength to customers who expect the highest possible financial security and integrity. John Hancock has been a leader in the institutional marketplace for over 50 years.

John Hancock Funds' Institutional Investments & Services group offers an innovative spectrum of high-quality asset management and administrative services to retirement plan sponsors and other institutional investors.

Investment Approach:
Disciplined investing using in-depth fundamental research, experienced in:

Active Equity Management
- International
- Small-Capitalization
- Sector Approach
- Value
- Growth

Active Fixed-Income Management
- Global and Domestic
- High-Yield

Service Approach
- A Targeted Approach Based on Industry Sector
- Investment Education & Communication Programs
- Daily Valuation Recordkeeping and Plan Administration
- Investment Management & Client Services
- Plan Design and Compliance
- Investment Advisory Services
- Trustee Services

KeyCorp

127 Public Square, Cleveland, OH 44114
Phone: 216-689-0391 • Fax: 216-689-3744
Toll Free: 800-982-3811, ext. 0391

Key Contacts:
Ann Leuth, *Director of*
 Product Management 216-689-0391
Donald Stone, *National Sales Manager* 216-689-1753

KeyCorp Assets Under Management: . . $50B*

DC Assets Under Administration: $16B*

DB/Other Institutional Assets
 Under Administration: $20B*
as of 12/31/96

Our KeyPRISM® daily valued 401(k) product offers the convenience of fully integrated services from a single, highly skilled source. This unique management program is designed specifically for 401(k) plans. Multifaceted in concept and design, KeyPRISM Daily provides a total spectrum of services, including investment management, trusteeship and administration services, participant recordkeeping and comprehensive employee education programs.

Beyond the standard daily valuation of assets, diversification of investments and automated participant telephone inquiry system, the KeyPRISM® Daily 401(k) also offers online access to your plan, management reports detailing plan participation and asset allocation, and paperless loan processing.

To achieve maximum return, we combine the capabilities of our portfolio managers with the advisory expertise of our entire trust and investment management organization. Our proprietary investment funds include the Key and Victory Funds, as well as collective funds including our premiere Key Trust EB MaGIC® collective investment trust. We also offer mutual fund offerings from Putnam Investments, Fidelity Advisor, Templeton, American Funds, Neuberger&Berman, AIM Institutional, INVESCO and Janus Funds. We can also accommodate publicly traded company stock funds in plans.

Each Plan Sponsor is backed by a comprehensive support network, led by their own Client Manager. All clients have access to the resources of more than 100 investment professionals, including Key Asset Management, Inc. — KeyCorp's leading registered investment adviser subsidiary, one of the largest equity research departments in the nation, with more than a dozen fixed-income specialists.

Merrill Lynch & Co.
Group Employee Services
800 Scudders Mill Road, Plainsboro, NJ 08536
Fax: 609-282-3891

Key Contacts:
Rene M. Campis, *First Vice President,*
Director, Sales and Client Service .. 609-282-3002
Gregory D. Upah, *First Vice President*
Merrill Lynch Asset Management ..609-282-2306

Total Qualified Retirement
Plan Assets: ....$74 billion

Plan Breakdown:
401(k) ....9,800 plans
Employee Stock Option ....22 plans
Employee Stock Purchase ....365 plans
Defined Benefit ....141 plans

Retirement Services: Group Employee Services, a fully integrated business unit of Merrill Lynch, is a premier provider of corporate retirement and employer-sponsored savings programs dedicated to serving the needs of our clients in a variety of employee benefit areas. With over 20 years of experience supporting employee benefit plan services, we bring together the investment expertise, state-of-the-art administrative capabilities, quality trust services and innovative communication and education programs required to help companies promote, implement and administer plans.

The Merrill Lynch Difference:
• Merrill Lynch provides superior investment flexibility to plan participants with the most comprehensive investment program offered in the marketplace. Participants may choose from an expanded menu of investment options offered by Merrill Lynch, as well as several brand name mutual fund families, making Merrill Lynch's product one of the most competitive in the industry. In addition, Merrill Lynch specializes in handling company stock as seamlessly as any other investment fund.
• The Communications and Education Services Group within Group Employee Services offers superior and award-winning programs for plan sponsors to offer participants.
• Our Participant Service Centers, located in Somerset, NJ, Denver, CO and by year-end 1997 Jacksonville FL, provide redundancies as well as contingency and recovery services unmatched in the industry.

MetLife
One Madison Avenue, New York, NY 10010

Key Contact:
Gary E. Lineberry, Vice President　　212-578-3181

Total Defined Contribution
Assets Under Management:　　$38.5 Billion*
* As of 12/31/96

The Informed (k)ˢᴹ Program:
Informed Choices for Retirement Planning

Services: The MetLife Informed (k) Program provides business owners with service levels that match their unique company needs. Sponsors can select standard or enhanced service, based on their own objectives and plan complexity. Recordkeeping and administrative services are provided by Benefit Services Corporation (BSC), a wholly owned subsidiary of MetLife. BSC provides efficient processing services for nearly 1,000 plans and 400,000 participants. BSC is distinguished by its commitment to quality and service provided by its staff of long-term employees.

Investments: Sponsors have access to a broad array of over 25 funding options, including some of today's best-known mutual fund families*, including: American Century, Founders, Janus, Loomis Sayles, Neuberger&Berman, Oakmark, PBHG, State Street Research and Warburg Pincus. Plan sponsors can also select from fixed-income options such as a guaranteed investment contract or a money market alternative. In addition, a series of pre-assembled asset allocation funds, sub-managed by United Asset Management, Inc. investment affiliates, are available to make investment decisions easier for less-experienced investors.

Communications: MetLife offers plan sponsors flexible communications materials which are targeted toward specific employee populations. Each one of our enrollment packages has been created to address a specific plan situation (e.g., new or existing plan) as well as to speak to different investment knowledge levels (e.g., new or experienced investors). Our standard educational package includes one of our pre-packaged enrollment kits, forms, announcement flyers, funding option fact sheets, performance information and an educational video. In addition, to supplement our standard communications offering, we offer an a la carte menu of optional services.

* *Available through group annuity contracts issued by Metropolitan Life Insurance Company. MetLife receives a fee from the fund families for providing certain recordkeeping and administrative services.*

Rogers, Casey & Associates, Inc.

One Parklands Drive, Darien, CT 06820
Phone 203-656-5900 • Fax 203-656-2233

Key Contacts:

Kenneth G. Rogers
Managing Director 203-656-5940

Lisa B. Stanton,
Managing Director 510-704-5061

Year Founded: 1976; wholly owned subsidiary
of BARRA, Inc.

Business Mission: Rogers, Casey & Associates,
Inc. offers products and services designed for the
investment programs of institutional investors. The
firm combines advanced technology and professional
relationship management to deliver investment
tools, consulting and special assets advisory (multi-
ple-manager programs).

Clients: RogersCasey services 150 institutional
investor clients — corporate and public funds,
endowments, foundations, hospitals, law firms,
insurance companies and unions — a client base
with combined assets of more than $500 billion.

Client Service: RogersCasey's experience is in the
design, implementation and monitoring of investment programs. A team approach allows clients to
access information and issue-solving capabilities
firmwide. Each client is assigned a relationship
team with accountability for day-to-day activities.
In addition, research specialists have responsibility
for coverage of specific asset classes. These specialists
are called upon as needed to assist with client
assignments.

Defined Contribution Consulting: RogersCasey
is a leader in the field of advising corporations on
how to structure and administer their Defined
Contribution plans. For example, a Strategic Review
project can be a cost-effective, focused way to determine priorities to improve participation rates, reduce
expenses and enhance the plan's performance.
RogersCasey can then also assist in fund selection,
ongoing performance monitoring and in designing
appropriate investment education materials.

Scudder Investor Services, Inc.

Two International Place, Boston, MA 02110-4103
Phone: (800) 541-7701 • Fax: (617) 443-7051

Key Contact Information:

Scott David, *Principal and Director of Defined
Contribution Sales* . . . . (800) 323-6105

Year Founded: 1919; Scudder, Stevens & Clark,
Inc. investment advisor to Scudder Funds. We
offered America's first *no-load* mutual funds in 1928.

**Total Assets Under Management From All
Sources:** . . . . In excess of $115 billion

Minimum Account Size: We service accounts of
all sizes, with an emphasis on plans with $5-$50
million in assets.

Special Areas of Expertise: Scudder Defined
Contribution Services provides *flexible* plan services,
including complete investment management, recordkeeping, employee education, and compliance and
trustee services. Scudder's full-service 401(k) capabilities enable our clients to effectively outsource as many
administrative functions as possible, educate participants on an ongoing basis, offer a full range of profes-
sionally managed investment options in each of the
desired asset classes, empower participants to effectively manage their accounts, and benefit from superi-
or, high-quality service. Scudder has provided defined
contribution plan services for more than 25 years, and
has been continuously committed to the 401(k) market for over a decade.

Frequency of Reporting Results: . . . . . Monthly

Assets Managed by Client Category:

	No. of clients managed	Assets (in millions)
Corporate Funds	150	$6,943
Public Funds	69	$8,464
Taft-Hartley Funds	27	$753
Endowments & Foundations	117	$2,247
Insurance	46	$5,156

* As of 9/30/96

Investment Approaches: Scudder follows a
disciplined and long-term investment approach
based on proprietary research by in-house analysts.
With a global approach to investing, the firm's 250+
investment professionals research and invest in
virtually every part of the world from offices and
affiliates in the U.S., Europe and Asia.

ANNOTATED BIBLIOGRAPHY
FINANCIAL PLANNING RESOURCES FOR ALL EMPLOYEEES

SUGGESTED READING

MAGAZINES AND NEWSPAPERS

Magazines and newspapers can provide timely information and advice on financial topics. Some general newspapers and magazines regularly covering personal finance and investing include: *Barron's, Investor's Business Daily, Business Week, USA Today, The Wall Street Journal* and *Consumer Reports Magazine*.

In addition, the following publications specialize in personal finance: *Kiplinger's Personal Finance Magazine, Money, Worth,* and *Smart Money*.

For a more offbeat approach, *Green: Personal Finance for the Unashamed*, offers basic financial advice aimed at young people.

BOOKS

➤ *Basic Investment Education:*
Dictionary of Finance and Investment Terms, 4th Edition, by John Downes and Jordan Elliot Goodman (Princeton, NJ: Barron's Educational Series, 1995). A valuable reference for quick information.

Economic Literacy: What Everyone Needs to Know About Money & Markets, by Jacob De Rooy (New York, NY: Crown, 1996). Clearly defines and illustrates fundamental economic principles, such as leading economic indicators, interest rates and monetary policy.

The Irwin Guide to Using The Wall Street Journal, 5th Edition, by Michael B. Lehmann (Burr Ridge, IL: Irwin Professional Publishing, 1996). A guide to using *The Wall Street Journal* to make informed investment choices. Topics include stocks, commodities, money market investments and interest rates.

The Wall Street Journal Guide to Understanding Money & Investing, by Kenneth Morris and Alan M. Siegel (New York, NY: Simon & Schuster, 1994). Covers all the basics: stocks, bonds, mutual funds, futures and money itself.

➤ *General Financial Planning Guides:*
The Beardstown Ladies' Stitch-In-Time Guide to Growing Your Nest Egg: Step-by-Step Planning for a Comfortable Financial Future, by the Beardstown Ladies Investment Club with Robin Dellabough (New York, NY: Hyperion, 1996). Offers basic financial information and advice on insurance, investments, 401(k) plans and more. Good book for young marrieds and recent college graduates.

The Consumer Reports Money Book: How to Get, Save and Spend it Wisely, by Janet Bamford, Jeff Blyskal, Emily Card and Aileen Jacobson (Yonkers, NY: Consumer Reports Books, 1995). Comprehensive reference book with helpful information on a wide range of topics, such as banking, taxes, insurance and investing.

Get a Financial Life: Personal Finance in Your Twenties and Thirties, by Beth Kobliner (New York, NY: Fireside, 1996). Excellent book for beginning investors and young professionals. Includes tips on buying a first home, refinancing high-interest debt and investing for retirement.

Kathy Kristof's Complete Book of Dollars and Sense: From Budget Basics to Lifetime Plans—The Only Guide You'll Need to Manage Your Money, by Kathy Kristof (New York, NY: Macmillan General Reference, 1997). "Sylvia Porter for the 90's" offers a simple, readable guide to organizing your finances and sorting through the tangle of bills and budget plans.

Left-Brain Finance for Right-Brain People: A Money Guide for the Creatively Inclined, by Paula Ann Monroe (Naperville, IL: Sourcebooks, Inc., 1996). Good financial primer, offering basic information on investments, taxes, insurance and retirement.

The Money Book of Personal Finance, by Richard Eisenberg and the editors at *Money* magazine (New York, NY: Warner Books, 1996). Contains tips on all aspects of money management, including home-buying, investments, taxes and insurance. Especially good resource for those who have complex finances.

Money: 127 Answers to Your Most-Asked Financial Questions: The Q&A Reference for Everything from Asset Allocation to Zero-Coupon Bonds, by Steven C. Camp (Fort Lauderdale, FL: Trunkey Publishing, 1995). Answers to commonly asked questions on a wide range of financial issues. Includes explanations of economic concepts, stocks and bonds, risk measurement and retirement plans.

The New York Times Personal Finance Handbook, by Leonard Sloane (New York, NY: Times Books, 1995). Comprehensive financial advice on a broad variety of topics, including mortgages, insurance, credit cards and investments.

Personal Finance for Dummies, by Eric Tyson (Foster City, CA: IDG Books Worldwide, Inc., 1994). An excellent book for novices, this non-intimidating primer covers everything from mutual funds and retirement planning to credit cards, spending reduction and insurance.

Price Waterhouse Personal Financial Adviser, by Price Waterhouse LLP (Burr Ridge, IL: Irwin Professional Publishing, 1995). Provides the framework for deciphering your financial goals and finding a balance between saving, spending and investing. Also covers financial planning for major life events, such as retirement, college, divorce and disability.

The Wall Street Journal Lifetime Guide to Money: Everything You Need to Know About Managing Your Finances—For Every Stage of Life, edited by C. Frederic Wiegold (New York, NY: Hyperion, 1997). Offers comprehensive information and advice on money management issues, including stock portfolios and debt management. Highlights important issues for people of various age groups.

Your Wealth-Building Years: Financial Planning for 18 to 38 Year Olds, 3rd edition, by Adriane G. Berg (New York, NY: Newmarket Press, 1995). Covers a wide range of topics, from cash flow and "pay-yourself-first" budgets to goal-setting and wealth-building strategies. Appropriate for young people earning $16,000 or more.

The Wealthy Barber, 2nd edition, by David Chilton (Rocklin, CA: Prima Publishing, 1996). Inspired by the television series "Cheers", a humorous novel in which a barber educates his customers about financial and retirement planning.

➤ *Special Interest Personal Finance Topics:*
The Black Woman's Guide to Financial Independence: Smart Ways to Take Charge of Your Money, Build Wealth, and Achieve Financial Security, by Cheryl D. Broussard (Newbern, TN: Penguin, USA, 1991, Reprint 1996). An easy-to-follow book that provides valuable advice on saving and investing.

Caring for Yourself While Caring for Your Aging Parents: How to Help, How to Survive, by Claire Berman (New York, NY: Henry Holt & Co., 1996). Explores a variety of issues facing adults who must care for two families at the same time. Includes information on financial aid and long distance care programs.

From Cradle to College: A Parent's Guide to Financing Your Child's Life, by Neale S. Godfrey with Ted Richards (New York, NY: Harper Business, 1996). Covers all financial aspects of parenting, such as housing, education and child care. Includes tables and forms used to determine a family's financial goals.

Credit Card and Debt Management: A Step-by-Step How-To Guide for Organizing Debts and Saving Money on Interest Payments, by Scott Bilker (Barnegat, NJ: Press One Publishing, 1996). Explains how to reduce debt, get the best credit card deals, determine true loan interest rates and calculate how much you can afford to borrow.

Managing Your Inheritance: Getting It, Keeping It, Growing It—Making the Most of Any Size Inheritance, by Emily Card and Adam Miller (New York, NY: Times Books, 1995). Guides new heirs through each stage of the inheritance process and gives advice on saving and investing wisely.

MoneySmart Divorce: What Women Need to Know about Money and Divorce, by Esther M. Berger (New York, NY: Simon & Schuster, 1996). Advice on managing finances before, during and after divorce and negotiating a "moneysmart" divorce settlement.

Smart Money Moves for African Americans, by Kelvin E. Boston (New York, NY: Putnam Publishing Group, 1996). Boston, a former financial adviser and host of syndicated television show, "The Color of Money," offers practical steps for increasing net worth, regardless of income or education level.

Two Incomes and Still Broke: It's Not How Much You Make, But How Much You Keep, by Linda Kelley Rouse (New York, NY: Times Books, 1996). Explains how to manage and maximize that second income and offers tips on reducing taxes.

Your Money Personality: What It Is and How You Can Profit from It, by Kathleen Gurney, Ph.D. (New York, NY: Doubleday, 1988). Dr. Gurney, Chairperson of the Financial Psychology Corporation, shows you how to identify your "money personality" and learn to make the most of it. Call (800) 735-7935.

➤ *Investment Guidance:*

The Beardstown Ladies' Common-Sense Investment Guide: How We Beat the Stock Market—And How You Can Too, by the Beardstown Ladies Investment Club (New York, NY: Hyperion, 1994). The club shares successful investment strategies with beginning investors.

The Craft of Investing: Growth and Value Stocks—Emerging Markets—Market Timing—Mutual Funds—Alternative Investments—Retirement and Estate Planning—Tax Savings, by John Train (New York, NY: Harper Business, 1995). Describes investment principles and strategies that are successful when used wisely.

How to Buy Bonds the Smart Way, by Stephen Littauer (Chicago, IL: Dearborn Trade, 1995). Explains how bonds and bond funds can help you achieve your investment goals and create a balanced portfolio.

The Motley Fool Investment Guide: How the Fool Beats Wall Street's Wise Men and How You Can Too, by David and Tom Gardner (New York, NY: Simon & Schuster, 1996). The men behind America Online's popular *"Motley Fool"*, an investment information forum, offer an entertaining, easy-to-read book on stock investing.

The Only Investment Guide You'll Ever Need, Revised and Updated, by Andrew Tobias (San Diego, CA: Harcourt Brace, 1996). In this revised version of a 1978 bestseller, respected personal finance expert Andrew Tobias, well-known for his humorous writing style, offers valuable advice on stocks, bonds, mutual funds and more.

The Portable MBA in Investment, edited by Peter L. Bernstein (New York, NY: John Wiley & Sons, Inc., 1996). Comprehensive analysis of investment principles and portfolio management. Industry experts examine investment goals and strategies, risk management and performance measurement.

A Random Walk Down Wall Street: The Best and Latest Investment Advice Money Can Buy, by Burton G. Malkiel (New York, NY: W.W. Norton & Company, 1996). In this 6th edition of a classic, Malkiel discusses the potential return on stocks and other investment vehicles. Also includes valuable information on home financing and insurance.

Scrooge Investing: The Bargain Hunter's Guide to More Than 120 Things You Can Do to Cut the Cost of Investing, by Mark Skousen (New York, NY: Little Brown & Co., 1996). Useful tips on how to make the most of your investment dollars. Advice on selecting a discount broker, postponing taxes and finding low-rate credit cards.

The 17 Laws of Successful Investing: Ignore Them at Your Own Risk, by Richard Rodman (Westfield, NJ: Alidan Press, 1996). Practical techniques to create more wealth.

The Whiz Kid of Wall Street's Investment Guide: How I Returned 34 Percent on My Portfolio and You Can, Too, by Matt Seto with Steven Levingston (New York, NY: William Morrow & Company, Inc., 1996). A good stock market primer from a 17-year old prodigy who created a private fund returning over 30% annual profit.

➤ *Mutual Fund Investing:*

Funding Your Future: The Only Guide to Mutual Funds You'll Ever Need, by Jonathan Clements (New York, NY: Warner Books, 1993). Clear explanations of mutual fund concepts and recommended portfolios for investors at different life stages.

Morningstar Mutual Fund 500 (Serial), by Morningstar, Inc. (Burr Ridge, IL: Irwin Professional Publishing, 1997). Full-page reports on 500 of the "most promising" mutual funds. Includes performance data, investment strategy and Morningstar's well-known star ratings.

Mutual Funds for Dummies, by Eric Tyson (Indianapolis, IN: IDG Books Worldwide, 1995). Another winner in the "Dummies" series, this entertaining book explains how to find the mutual funds that best suit your needs.

Mutual Fund Investing on the Internet: The Ultimate Guide to Mutual Fund Trading and Information Online, by Peter G. Crane (San Diego, CA: AP Professional, 1997). Shows you how to find and use the best financial information on the Web. Also guides you through mutual fund basics and investment strategies.

The 100 Best Mutual Funds You Can Buy: Includes Money Market Funds, by Gordon K. Williamson (Holbrook, MA: Adams Publishing, 1996). Provides detailed reviews of top stock, bond and money market funds in 13 categories. Analyzes total return, risk, current income, management quality and expense control.

➤ *Retirement and 401(k) Plans:*

Building Your Nest Egg With Your 401(k), by Lynn Brenner (Washington Depot, CT: Investors Press, 1995). The definitive guide for 401(k) participants and eligible enrollees.

Escaping the Coming Retirement Crisis: How to Secure Your Financial Future, by R. Theodore Benna and William Proctor (Colorado Springs, CO: Pinon Press, 1995). Ted Benna, "father of the 401(k) plan", offers valuable guidelines and advice on investing for retirement.

Helping Employees Achieve Retirement Security, by Ted Benna (Washington Depot, CT; Investors Press, 1995). A comprehensive guide to 401(k) plans that answers more than 100 of the most frequently asked employee questions.

The 401(k) Book: Your Last Best Hope for Retirement Savings! by Richard Sasanow (New York, NY: Henry Holt, 1996). Clearly explains 401(k) plan rules and investment strategies.

Retiring Right: Planning for a Successful Retirement, by Lawrence J. Kaplan (New York, NY: Avery, 1990). Advice on the financial aspects of retirement, including housing, health care and Social Security.

Secure Your Future: Your Personal Companion for Understanding Lifestyle & Financial Aspects of Retirement, by Price Waterhouse, LLP (Burr Ridge, IL: Irwin Professional Publishing, 1995). Helps answer questions, such as when to retire, what kind of lifestyle you want and what investment return is needed to achieve your goals. Useful for readers of any age.

Standard & Poor's 401(k) Planning Guide, by Alan J. Miller (New York, NY: McGraw-Hill, 1994). How to make maximum use of your 401(k) plan, including tips on evaluating investments and monitoring performance.

➤ *Taxes:*

Consumer Reports Books: Guide to Income Taxes, by Warren H. Esanu, Barry Dickman and Elias M. Zuckerman (Yonkers, NY: Consumer Reports Books, 1997). Annual tax preparation guide, including a helpful organizer work sheet.

J.K. Lasser's Your Income Tax, by J.K. Lasser Institute (New York, NY: Macmillan General Reference, 1996). A comprehensive, step-by-step tax guide, covering almost every conceivable situation.

Taxes for Dummies, by Eric Tyson and David J. Silverman (Indianapolis, IN: IDG Books Worldwide, 1996). Explains tax codes in plain English.

VIDEOS

Kiplinger Washington Editors, Inc., the publishers of *Kiplinger's Personal Finance Magazine*, provide a series of money management videos and guidebooks, including "Family Finances", "Mutual Funds", and "Retirement Security". Call (800) 727-7015.

Saving & Investing, an informative videotape sponsored by the Federal Reserve Board and the Securities and Exchange Commission. Expert discussion and advice on budgeting, banking and investing. Call Vidicopy at (800) 708-7080.

TELEVISION PROGRAMS

Two notable television programs that provide timely financial news and market analysis for individual investors are:

The Money Wheel (CNBC)
Wall Street Week (PBS)

INVESTMENT RESEARCH PUBLICATIONS

➤ *Mutual Funds:*

Morningstar, a comprehensive source of mutual fund information and analysis, provides regularly updated publications that include detailed research reports and their famous star ratings for a vast number of mutual and closed-end funds. Below is a list of some of their publications. For more information, call (800) 735-0700.

Morningstar Investor: Offers market analysis and strategies to help you create your portfolio. Also provides detailed reports on the "Morningstar 500", 500 of the most promising mutual and closed-end funds.

Morningstar No-Load Funds: Provides full-page reports on 690 top no-load and low-load mutual funds. Includes analyst reviews, performance graphs and manager biographies.

Morningstar Mutual Funds Report: Provides 1,500 full-page fund reports, including written analysis of each funds' strengths and weaknesses. For serious investors.

Note: If you just need reports on a few funds, the Morningstar OnDemand service can mail or fax them to you for $5 per report.

➤ Stocks:

Moody's Handbook of Common Stock (NYSE), by Moody's Investors Service: Provides detailed reports on New York Stock Exchange companies. Includes company news, performance statistics and Moody's long and short-term forecasts. Call (800) 342-5647, ext. 0546.

Value Line Investment Survey, by Value Line, Inc.: Provides statistics and analysis of approximately 1,700 of the most actively traded stocks. Includes "Timeliness" and "Safety" rankings for each stock. Call (800) 634-3583.

INFORMATION FROM ORGANIZATIONS AND GOVERNMENT AGENCIES

➤ General Personal Finance:

American Association of Retired Persons (AARP), (800) 424-3410, offers free publications on money management and retirement issues for individuals of all ages.

American Savings Education Council (ASEC), part of the Employee Benefit Research Institute (EBRI) Education and Research Fund, offers information on the importance of saving and planning: *The Power to Choose, How Do I Get There From Here?* and *Top 10 Ways to Beat the Clock and Prepare for Retirement.* To order these free publications, send a self-addressed, #10 envelope with 55¢ postage to Suite 600, 2121 K Street NW, Washington, DC 20037-1896 or call (202) 659-0670.

The Consumer Information Center provides a free catalog listing more than 200 Federal publications on a wealth of topics, including money management, home financing and credit. Call (719) 948-4000 or write to: Catalog, Consumer Information Center, Pueblo, CO 81009.

Investing:

American Association of Individual Investors (AAII), (800) 428-2244, a non-profit organization, offers many investment education materials for both beginning and advanced investors. Annual membership is $49 per year.

The Federal Reserve Bank of NY offers information on purchasing Treasury Securities directly, without a broker. Call (212) 720-6130 to order the *First-Time Buyers' Treasury Securities Kit,* which provides purchasing information and forms. To learn about savings bonds, call (617) 565-6100 to order " U.S. Savings Bond Investor Information" (Publication #SB2192), which offers general information about the features and benefits of savings bonds.

Investment Company Institute, a trade group of the mutual fund industry, provides a catalog of free consumer publications, such as *What is a Mutual Fund?* and *Reading the Mutual Fund Prospectus.* For $8.50, you can also order the *Directory of Mutual Funds,* which provides toll-free telephone numbers and financial data on member mutual funds. Call (202) 326-5800 or write to 1401 H Street, NW, Suite 1200, Washington, DC 20005-2148.

The Securities and Exchange Commission, (800) SEC-0330, provides free, informative brochures on investing, including: *Invest Wisely*, which explains how to choose brokers and investments; *Invest Wisely: An Introduction to Mutual Funds*, which describes how mutual funds work; and *What Every Investor Should Know*, which covers the fundamentals of securities investing.

Securities Industry Association (SIA), a trade group of securities firms, offers **Your Guide to Understanding Investing,** a 179-page investment primer filled with useful information about investing from how to read financial data in the newspaper to analyses of the uses, risks and rewards of specific investment products. To order, send $13.95 to: 120 Broadway, 35th Floor, New York, NY 10271-0080, Attn. Guide, or call (212) 618-0534.

➤ *Pensions and Retirement Planning:*

Pension Education Clearinghouse provides a listing of consumer publications on pensions and retirement income. Send a self-addressed, business-size envelope with 55¢ postage to P.O. Box 19821, Washington, DC 20036.

Pension and Welfare Benefits Administration provides consumers with the information needed to protect their benefit rights. Call (202) 219-9247 or contact the PWBA office nearest you.

➤ *Credit:*

BankCard Holders of America (BHA), (540) 389-5445, a non-profit consumer protection organization, provides credit information and advice. Write to BHA, 524 Branch Drive, Salem, VA 24153, for a free publications list or send $4 for a list of low-rate, no fee credit card issuers.

The Federal Trade Commission (FTC), (202) 326-2222, offers a free *Best Sellers Brochure* listing its most popular consumer education publications on topics such as credit cards, credit problems and home financing.

The National Foundation for Consumer Credit, (800) 388-2227, can refer you to local Consumer Credit Counseling Service (CCCS) agencies—non-profit organizations offering counseling for serious debt problems.

➤ *Taxes:*

The Internal Revenue Service offers **Your Federal Income Tax,** a free 300+ page guide providing detailed instructions on filling out tax forms and a listing of other helpful IRS publications. Call (800) TAX-FORM and ask for Publication 17.

Federal Programs and Benefits:

The following publications can be ordered from the Social Security Administration at (800) 772-1213:

The Medicare Handbook, a 64-page resource that explains who is eligible, how to apply and fill out claims, what is and isn't covered and your right to appeal.

Request for Earnings and Benefit Estimate Statement, a form you submit to the Social Security Administration to receive an estimate of your Social Security benefits in retirement. Order an application by phone or apply online: www.ssa.gov.

Social Security: What Every Woman Should Know, a 15-page pamphlet that explains benefits upon retirement, disability, widowhood and divorce.

Understanding Social Security, a 41-page pamphlet that explains retirement, disability, survivor's benefits, Medicare coverage, Supplemental Security Income and more.

FINANCIAL PLANNERS:

➤ *Information:*

Facts About Financial Planners, by the AARP, explains what you can expect from different types of financial planning professionals and provides a list of questions you should ask prospective candidates. Access via the Internet at: www.pueblo.gsa.gov/cic_text/money/planner.txt, or write to: AARP Fulfillment, 601 E Street NW, Washington, DC 20049.

Worth magazine (October 1996), published a list of the credentials and phone numbers for the 200 "Best Financial Advisers" in the United States.

Organizations:

The Institute of Certified Financial Planners, (800) 282-PLAN, provides information and referrals on financial planners throughout the country, many of whom offer education and seminar programs.

American Institute of Certified Public Accountants, (800) 862-4272, provides a list of CPAs who are also personal finance specialists.

SOFTWARE

The following software programs are available in local software chains, such as Egghead Software and CompUSA. Be sure to get the latest editions of the software.

➤ *Cash management:*

Cash management programs are valuable tools for organizing your finances and figuring out where your money is going. Here are three of the best:

Quicken, by Intuit, (800) 446-8848.
Managing Your Money, by MECA Software, (800) 288-6322.
Microsoft Money, by Microsoft Corporation, (800) 426-9400.

Taxes:

The following tax preparation programs help you file more easily and offer tax planning advice:

Turbo Tax, for Windows, by Intuit, (800) 446-8848.
Mac-in-Tax, for Macs, by Intuit, (800) 446-8848.
Kiplinger TaxCut, by Block Financial Corporation, (800) 235-4060.

➤ *Financial planning and investing research:*

Investor Insight, by Intuit, (800) 446-8848. An easy-to-use investment information service. For investors with large stock portfolios, it provides company news, charting and personalized research reports.

Quicken Financial Planner 2, by Intuit, (800) 446-8848. Helps you create a personal financial plan for retirement, college-financing, home-buying and more.

Morningstar Ascent, by Morningstar, Inc., (800) 735-0700. Provides detailed analysis of over 7,000 mutual funds, which can be searched and ranked based on 70 characteristics, including historical performance, risk scores and Morningstar's star ratings.

Reuters Money Network, by Reality Online, (800) 521-2475. A combination investment software and online service, offering quotes, personalized news reports and stock, bond and mutual fund data.

Web Sites

Warning: When using the Internet to obtain investment information, please consider the reliability of the source. The National Association of Security Dealers Regulation, Inc. has published a worthwhile article on using Internet information wisely; you can access this article, "Possibilities and Pitfalls: The Internet As An Investment Tool", at: www.nasdr.com.

➤ *General Financial Planning:*
CNNfn: The Financial Network, (cnnfn.com). Features market news, stock quotes and a personal finance section entitled "Your Money".

Kiplinger Online, (www.kiplinger.com). Personal finance articles, daily market news and business forecasts.

The Los Angeles Times, (www.latimes.com). Personal finance columnist Kathy Kristof offers helpful explanations and advice on a wide range of personal investing and financial planning topics.

Money Personal Finance Center, (www.moneymag.com). Selected articles from *Money* magazine and also "Money Daily", a one-page summary of daily business and investment news.

Worth OnLine, (www.worth.com). Excerpts of *Worth* magazine and a full archive of back issues, including all of legendary Peter Lynch's columns.

➤ *Assorted Personal Finance Topics:*
Bank Rate Monitor's Infobank, (www.bankrate.com). Prevailing interest rates on CDs, mortgages, loans and credit cards. Updated weekly listings in approximately 100 cities nationwide.

FinAid: The Financial Aid Information Page, (www.finaid.com). A wealth of financial aid and scholarship information for parents of college-age children.

Legal Documents, (www.legaldocs.com). USA Law Publications provides free interactive wills and estate planning documents. The "required reading" section explains the basics of estate and will planning.

Sallie Mae, (www.salliemae.com). Sallie Mae, a provider of funds for education loans, offers valuable financial aid information, including useful calculators for estimating college costs and financing needs.

➤ *Investment Tools and Information:*

INVESTools, (www.investools.com). Research on funds and stocks. For a fee, you can download a variety of newsletters or reports, such as Standard & Poor's Stock Reports.

Morningstar.Net, (www.morningstar.net). Professional-quality data and analysis on over 7,000 funds. The "X-Ray" section helps you assess the riskiness of your portfolio and see how your holdings fit together.

Mutual Funds Investors Center, (www.mfea.com). Information on almost every aspect of mutual fund investing for novices. The "Get Educated" section explains all the basics.

NetWorth, (www.networth.galt.com). Provides stock and fund information. Search through fund data by specifying factors of interest to you.

Stock Smart, (www.stocksmart.com). Offers stock research data. Compare specific companies to industry-group peers and track the value of your investments.

Workplace Fidelity, (wps.fidelity.com). A section of the Fidelity Online Investment Center Web site dedicated to workplace retirement plans. Includes retirement planning worksheets, investment education for novices and market commentary by Fidelity analysts.

➤ *Online Services:*

You need not confine your search to the World Wide Web. Major online service providers also offer proprietary sites and portfolio-tracking capabilities. For example, America Online provides access to selected Morningstar reports, while Prodigy's Stock Hunter allows you to select and research stocks for an additional fee. To check their latest offerings, call **AOL,** (800)827-6364, **Prodigy,** (800) 776-3449 and **CompuServe,** (800) 848-8199.

➤ *Organizations and Government Agencies:*

AAII: American Association of Individual Investors, (www.aaii.org). Educational material for both beginning and advanced investors.

American Association of Retired Persons, (www.aarp.org). Information on money management and retirement planning, as well as a wealth of information for retirees and their caregivers.

American Bankers Association, (www.aba.com). A "Personal Finance" area educates consumers using useful calculators to aid decision-making about mortgages, auto loans and more.

American Savings Education Council, (www.asec.org). Educational materials to help you plan and achieve your savings goals. Includes informative publications, definitions of financial terms and links to other helpful resources.

Consumer Information Center, (www.pueblo.gsa.gov). An excellent site for personal finance information. Visit the "Money" section for information on financial planners, pensions, credit cards, investing tips and more.

Federal Reserve Bank of NY, (www.ny.frb.org). Valuable information on U.S. Savings Bonds, U.S. Treasuries and Notes, including instructions on how to buy them directly and compute the redemption values for a savings bond.

FTC Consumer Brochures, (www.webcom.com). Informative brochures published by the FTC's Office of Consumer and Business Education on topics such as credit cards, credit problems and home financing.

Internal Revenue Service, (www.irs.ustreas.gov/prod/cover.html). User-friendly site provides tax regulations, forms and publications.

Pension and Welfare Benefits Administration, (www.dol.gov/dol/pwba). Useful publications on pensions. Topics include: preparing for retirement, your pension rights and claiming your benefits.

Securities and Exchange Commission, (www.sec.gov). The SEC's Office of Investor Education and Assistance offers worthwhile information on investing wisely and avoiding securities fraud.

Social Security Administration, (www.ssa.gov). Provides helpful publications explaining Social Security programs and benefits.

SUGGESTIONS FROM THE UNDERWRITERS

➤ **Allmerica Financial** suggests:

Ernst & Young's Personal Financial Planning Guide: **Take Control of Your Future and Unlock the Door to Financial Security**, by Robert Coplan and Robert J. Garner. (New York, NY: John Wiley & Sons, 1995).

The Financially Independent Woman: A Step-By-Step Guide to Successful Investing, by Barbara Lee (Wausau, WI: Birch Lane Press, 1996).

The Wall Street Journal Guide to Planning Your Financial Future, by Alan M. Siegel, Kenneth Morris and Virginia Morris (New York, NY: Fireside Publishing, 1995).

Estate and Financial Planning: Making Your Money Work Harder, by Paul R. Hinrichs, Ph.D. (Arlington, TX: Now Books, 1995).

The Financial Planning Manual: Complete Approach to Estate and Retirement Planning, by Paul R. Hinrichs, Ph.D. (Arlington, TX: Now Books, 1995).

➤ **American Century**$_{SM}$ **Investments** offers the following resources. Fax your request to 816-340-7932.

Focusing on the Basics: How to Choose Your Plan Provider identifies six basic areas to consider when choosing your plan provider and helps you rate prospects. A sample Request for Proposal, as well as guidelines for reference checks and site visits are included.

Keeping it Simple: 12 Ways to Make Enrollment Easier highlights findings from the qualitative participant research that influenced the development of our enrollment materials.

Insights and Issues is a quarterly newsletter for defined contribution plan sponsors. It provides information on legislative and administrative issues affecting qualified retirement plans plus retirement trends and communications issues.

➤ **Founders'** educational materials include the following papers, contact; Greg Contillo, 800-806-2986.

A Guide to Growth Stock Investing. Growth stock investing is an approach that has rewarded investors over time and across many economic cycles. This free educational guide discusses the characteristics of growth stocks, how money managers find them and the potential advantages they offer long-term investors.

Preparing Your Portfolio for Uncertain Markets. The stock market, while breaking records in recent years, has experienced wide swings of volatility. What would a sustained market drop mean to long-term investors? This free educational guide discusses options a stock fund investor may wish to consider in uncertain markets.

Passport to International Investing. With today's global marketplace, you have many opportunities to profit from foreign investments. A free brochure from Founders discusses the long-term growth and diversification opportunities of investing overseas.

Making the Grade. Children grow up in the blink of an eye. Unfortunately, it often takes longer to save for college. A free guide to help parents plan for one of the most valuable assets their child will ever own—a college education.

➤ **John Hancock Funds** recommends:

"Participant Attitudes on Retirement Saving"—a defined contribution plan survey done periodically by John Hancock Financial Services and the Gallup Organization. This survey evaluates the opinions and attitudes of employees currently contributing to a 401(k) or equivalent retirement plan. To order, call 1-800-755-4371.

➤ **KeyCorp** suggests:

Key's extensive educational library of booklets, videos and seminars on topics such as *Basics of Investing, Asset Allocation, Mutual Fund Basics, Understanding Mutual Fund Benchmarks, Ratings & Rankings* and *Retirement Planning for Women*—all designed to help employees acquire good saving and investing disciplines. Applicable for both 401(k) investing and other personal financial goals. Call 800-982-3811, ext. 4347.

➤ **MetLife** suggests:

"Phooey on Mutual Funds," Janice Koch, *Institutional Investor,* September 1996. Some 401(k) plan sponsors think mutual funds are not worth the high fees; instead, they are turning to cheaper alternatives, such as separate and commingled accounts.

"Addressing a Long-Neglected Issue, Some Large Defined Contribution Plans are Demanding Greater Compliance with Investment Guidelines," Susan Arterian, *Plan Sponsor,* July-August 1996. More and more defined contribution plans are demanding style purity and adherence to investment guidelines.

"Custom Fit," moderated by Judy Ward, *Plan Sponsor,* April 1996. One standardized approach does not entice all employees to participate in defined contribution plans. This article highlights how plan sponsors approach five groups of employees with special needs.

➤ **RogersCasey** offers an internally produced paper on:

"Considerations in the Design of Investment Options for Defined Contribution Plans," by Anne C. Buehl and Robin S. Pellish, April 1997. Contact: Karen Dehmel at 203-656-5900.

➤ **Scudder, Stevens & Clark, Inc.** recommends the following resources. Contact Bill Hynes, (617) 295-3021:

"University Focuses Scudder's 401(k) Educational Effort," Meghan Kinney, *Employee Benefit News,* October 1996. Insights to how interactive, educational programs have helped 401(k) plan sponsors reach their plan participation and asset allocation goals.

"The Case For International Investing," by Nicholas Bratt, Director of Global Equity Group, Scudder, Stevens & Clark, Inc. The author discusses how international investing automatically affords the possibility of exposure to broad investment opportunities while providing instant diversification and the ability to exploit different opportunities and risks.

YOUR EMPLOYEES MAY HAVE A FEW QUESTIONS ABOUT THEIR 401(k) PLAN

We Have More Than 100 Answers

I t's not surprising that plan participants have lots of questions about their 401(k) plan: how it works; what they can expect to withdraw from it and when; how to make the most sensible investments for their specific needs; whether or not they should even enroll.

As evidence mounts that employees are not investing early enough, wisely enough or simply *enough*, plan sponsors have an increasingly urgent obligation to give their employees a solid basis for making sound decisions about their financial future.

That's why this book from Investors Press is so important.

A New Way to Boost Plan Enrollment

Written specifically for plan participants and eligible enrollees, **Building Your Nest Egg With Your 401(k)** gives them the confidence and knowledge they need to manage their 401(k). In concise, *easy-to-understand* language, this important new book answers more than a hundred of the most commonly asked employee questions about 401(k)s. These independent, objective responses will help your employees make more informed judgments about the value of enrolling early, the maximum amount they should save and which investment

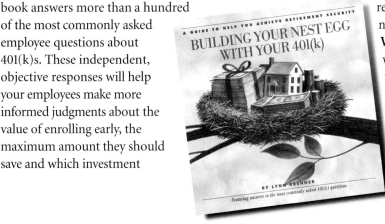

vehicles will best help them meet their specific needs and expectations. Throughout this handsome book's 160 pages, 4-color tables, charts and graphs illustrate and explain key aspects of saving and investing. Thorough and entirely relevant to participants' practical needs, **Building Your Nest Egg With Your 401(k)** is also an ideal way for plan sponsors to comply with 404(c) voluntary guidelines. This ground breaking book provides the impartial, third-party information participants need to plan for a secure retirement.

SEEKING INNOVATIVE WAYS TO COMMUNICATE
TOTAL FINANCIAL PLANNING IDEAS TO YOUR EMPLOYEES?

Reprints of two valuable sections of this book, Beyond the 401(k): Helping Employees Achieve Total Financial Security, are available in bulk quantities. For more information, please check the appropriate boxes below:

- Annotated Bibliography: "Financial Planning Resources for All Employees" (see pages 85-98)

- "Employee Communications: Top Tips on Saving, Investing and Spending from Leading Financial Planners Nationwide" (see pages 72-79)

☐ I am interested in a quantity of _____ (minimum 50).

_____
NAME

_____
COMPANY

_____
PHONE   FAX

(BEY)

BUSINESS REPLY MAIL
FIRST CLASS MAIL   PERMIT NO. 10   WASHINGTON DEPOT, CT

POSTAGE WILL BE PAID BY ADDRESSEE

INVESTORS PRESS BOOKS
P.O. BOX 329
WASHINGTON DEPOT, CT 06794-9809